WITHDRAWN

COMPARISONS IN ART

A Companion to the
National Gallery of Art
Washington · DC

'DIANE DE POITIERS.' By François Clouet

COMPARISONS IN ART

A COMPANION TO
THE NATIONAL GALLERY OF ART
WASHINGTON · DC

by FERN RUSK SHAPLEY

Assistant Chief Curator
National Gallery of Art

WITH INTRODUCTORY ESSAYS
by JOHN SHAPLEY

Professor of Art and Archaeology
Catholic University of America

PHAIDON PUBLISHERS INC
DISTRIBUTED BY DOUBLEDAY AND CO · INC
NEW YORK · 1959

First published in 1957
Second printing 1959

Made in Great Britain
Printed by Geo Gibbons Ltd · Leicester

CONTENTS

To

BERNARD BERENSON

" . . . reaching out to the topmost peak
of our capacities, contented with no
satisfaction lower than the highest."

Aesthetics and History

PREFACE

IF it is true that the pleasures of anticipation and of recollection make up most of the joy of life, then this book may promise to bring its contribution. For it is designed to prepare future visitors for their prospective experiences in the National Gallery and to recall to past visitors the impressions they have already garnered. Nor is that all. Illuminating ideas which otherwise might never dawn may arise spontaneously when it is possible, in reproductions, to isolate and confront details or to view side by side objects that are widely separated in exhibition galleries.

To exploit as fully as possible these advantages of the printed reproduction, plates are here arranged in pairs. The pairing is prompted by some revelation it offers regarding style, purpose, or other matter; and the result of the confrontation is discussed in text printed on the plates themselves. Sometimes a piece of sculpture gives up its secret when we compare it with a painting of the same period. Sometimes a pertinent thought springs to mind the moment we see together two works of widely different periods. It may prove profitable to study an Italian painting along with a Dutch painting, or the work of a certain artist beside that of his closest associate. So fascinating are the opportunities for fruitful comparison that one wishes it were possible to present the plates in more than one arrangement, thus provoking new comparisons and further appreciation of the treasures represented.

This approach to art through comparison has been facilitated by grouping the plates under the following six categories: religious art, mythology and allegory, portraiture, *genre, still life, and landscape. An introductory essay is devoted to each category.*

The works of art reproduced on the plates are all chosen from the collections of the National Gallery of Art. Some of the illustrations to the introductory essays are drawn from elsewhere.

* * *

We wish to record here our appreciation of the late Dr. B. Horovitz, Director of the Phaidon Press, 'a most vital, cultured, and entertaining man, and the most enterprising and adventurous of publishers,' as Bernard Berenson has characterized him. It was at the suggestion of Dr. Horovitz, and with his encouragement and approval, that this book was written.

F.R.S. & J.S.

RELIGIOUS ART

For our purpose of setting in perspective those works of art illustrated in this volume, the only religious art to be considered is Christian and of the current millennium. This art shares the general obligation of religious art to be worthy of the holiness associated with it. To achieve such worthiness the use of the best materials the world affords is called for, as a tribute to the divine.

Suger's chalice (Pl. 1) is an example of the fulfilment of these exacting requirements. Into its mounting went precious metals—gold and silver, precious stones—rubies, emeralds, and jades, and numerous specimens of the traditional symbol of the most precious—the pearl. The bowl, which was thus luxuriously mounted, represented to the good Abbot Suger an even greater offering at the altar: being sardonyx, it was precious; but being an antique, it was a rarity not to be duplicated, as the metals and gems might have been.

The gold-and-enameled morse studded with pearls (Pl. 8) offers a comparable display of dazzling materials. In fact, throughout the Christian centuries the claim of religious art to maximum material outlay has been recognized, from the gold glass of the catacombs to the glittering mosaics of today. Hence we have the Early Christian church silver, the sumptuary arts of Byzantium, the gold ground of miniatures, mosaics, and panel paintings.

It is not surprising that the ceiling of S. Maria Maggiore is said to have been gilt with the first gold to arrive from America, or that the chapel of the canonized author of the *Spiritual Exercises* in the first Jesuit church in Rome, the Gesù, was provided with four large columns of lapis lazuli flanking a silver statue of St. Ignatius, and that the largest known block of lapis lazuli was added, high above. For the ideal of material worthiness is inseparable from Christian religious art.

The gold background tended to fall into disuse at the end of the Middle Ages for a whole complex of reasons, including greater interest in worldly things, economy, and the desire to make the spiritual more accessible and convincing. But though the trend was away from the gold background, good materials were still stipulated. Subsequent neglect of them, increasing from the Renaissance onward, proved most harmful to religious art.

No less insistent than the demand for worthy material in religious art is the demand for worthy workmanship. It is often mentioned, in one way or another, in old contracts. Minute refinement, as seen in the Madonnas here illustrated, is in recognition of this demand. Even today the touchstone of good workmanship conveniently differentiates religious art from what are called religious articles.

Works of Christian religious art have traditionally been admirable as objects, irrespective of what they might represent or how they might be intended for use.

It is repeatedly said that representation in Christian art was motivated by the desire to instruct the unlettered. The truth is that the unlettered were made familiar with the subject matter of art through the daily readings and teachings of the Church. Sculptures and pictures merely provided visual illustration of what the common man knew already. They furnished visualizations to correspond with verbalizations. In the important mediaeval art of manuscript painting the illustrations were obviously addressing the lettered, who had access to the manuscripts. The relics of older religious art seem far more didactic to us today than they were to their contemporaries.

Two capital aspects of the whole great theme of salvation have been emergent in Christian art. They are the Incarnation and the Redemption. The former was most effectively expressed by the Virgin with the Infant Christ (the Madonna); the latter, by the Crucifixion. The two subjects have such a dominating position that they call for prolonged attention here.

The Madonna had figured in art for about a thousand years before the earliest examples in the National Gallery were painted. The central rôle in Christianity of the Mother of God was officially

Fig. 1. MARGARITONE:
Madonna and Child
Enthroned

formalized at the Council of Ephesus in 431, but this act doubtless represented a *post facto* confirmation of what was already widely accepted regarding her. From soon thereafter we begin to have preserved works in which she is handsomely enthroned, as she is in the Gallery's earliest Madonnas, of the thirteenth century.

Enthroned Madonnas of the thirteenth century have been classified by iconographers as of three types. This classification obviously has to disregard many variations. It is convenient to call the types by Byzantine names: (1) the Blacherniotissa, (2) the Hodegetria, (3) the Glykophilousa. This is the order of their historical sequence, both as to effective dispersion and presumptive origin, in the Christian East, and as to subsequent rise to popularity in the West. The advent of one type did not, of course, mean the extinction of its predecessor.

The Blacherniotissa (Fig. 1) has the Virgin seated frontally and usually on a low throne without back. She is full-length. Normally the Child is shown frontally before the Virgin, and raises His right hand in blessing. Distinctive of this type is its ceremonial otherworldliness, which suits it to formal altarpieces. The name derives from the convent of Blachernae at Constantinople, where there seems to have been a famous Madonna of this type. The Blacherniotissa had already reached the West in Early Christian times. It went out of regular use in the fourteenth century, but there are later archaistic examples and occasional revivals.

The Hodegetria (Pl. 2) did not effectively penetrate the West until well along in the Middle Ages. Perhaps originally abstractly conceived as 'She who shows the Way,' it was concretized as 'She

3

Fig. 2. FLORENTINE, LATE XIII CENTURY:
Madonna and Child with Saints.
Birmingham, Alabama,
Birmingham Museum of Art

who points the Way.' This type presents the Virgin holding the
Child on her left arm and reaching ('pointing') toward Him with
her right. He raises His right hand. The two figures are turned
more or less toward one another, on a throne that is normally high-
backed, and the Virgin's head is regularly in something like three-
quarters view and usually tilted. Toward the end of the Middle
Ages this type became more and more dominant, and with endless
variations it has continued to flourish through the centuries. In
late examples the relative position of the figures is freely reversed,
and the group is frequently half-length.

The Glykophilousa (Fig. 2) is little more than a variant of the
Hodegetria, from which it is clearly derivative. Its iconographic
isolation gives us at least a resounding name, which means 'She
who is sweetly loving.' In this type the Virgin and the Child are in
intimate relationship. Instead of blessing, the Child commonly

4

puts His arm around His mother's neck and presses His face against hers. It is normally a half-length type and suitable for more familiar surroundings.

At the risk of exemplifying Aristotle's 'frigidity'—that is, the far-fetched—a sort of parallel of the three types of Madonnas to the orders of Greek architecture may be mentioned. The Blacherniotissa has some correspondence to the Doric. It is dignified, formal, and accordingly somewhat lacking in adaptability. The more lively Hodegetria and Glykophilousa recall the Ionic and Corinthian. In both cases the second derives from the first.

As it often does in life, so in the iconography of the Madonna, adaptability outran dignity. The more and more materialized Madonnas of later times, often with feeding, playing, and other nursery motives, derive from the Hodegetria and Glykophilousa types.

How the Hodegetria outlived the centuries is illustrated in the fifteenth-century example by Gentile da Fabriano (Pl. 4). With the Virgin's right hand definitely helping to support the Child, her traditional reaching gesture has become more specific and more maternal. The Child's right hand is more babyish, and the motive of blessing quite submerged. In a word, the abstraction of the older Hodegetria is almost gone, and along with it has receded its aloofness. The latter change is conveniently measured by the declining importance of the throne. Despite the setting and the costumes and the religious subject, we are now in the nursery, where the tethered butterfly is not out of place, whatever recondite signification pundits would read into the gay insect.

The low throne of the Madonna had been a characteristic of the oldest enthroned type, the Blacherniotissa (Fig. 1). Deep in the Renaissance, about 1460, in a Madonna of Cosimo Tura (Pl. 35) this type is implicit. Tura shows the Virgin in the abstraction of prayer, expressed by her hands. The Child is before her, precariously perched between her knees, and asleep though not reclining. The background is formal, basically a verdure screen. But the Child's sleeping is an incongruous Renaissance touch of the nursery.

5

What could happen in the course of time to the Glykophilousa is shown by a Madonna of Carlo Crivelli (Pl. 12). True to type it is a half-length, but now the Child is standing on a ledge. The ledge, like the fruit and the flowered embroidery, is regarded as something coming into Italy from the North. Perhaps the reversal of the position of the figures, frequent after the middle of the fifteenth century, is connected with the reversal that the making of prints readily leads to. The reversal had the advantage, illustrated in Crivelli's Glykophilousa, of allowing a clinging Child to bless with His right hand. It did not enter into sculpture so much as into painting. In general, sculptors would presumably be less vulnerable than painters to the influence of prints. The not much earlier half-length Madonna by Agostino di Duccio (Pl. 11), for instance, is still an unreversed and wholly standard example of the half-length Hodegetria, however much Agostino and other Florentine sculptors of his time were anxiously emulating painting, which had in their generation taken the lead away from sculpture.

Such subjects as the Madonna of Humility and the Flight into Egypt encouraged the painting of Madonnas seated in a landscape. These Madonnas were less constrained by iconographical habits because they were independent of the old traditions of enthroned Madonnas. The Rest on the Flight by Gerard David (Pl. 25) illustrates how a Virgin and Child presented in this less ceremonial connection could be shown busying themselves, as freely as St. Joseph in the background, with the concerns of everyday life. It was *de rigueur*, however, that the attitudes be decorous. Hence the monumental, nearly frontal pose of David's Madonna. And the attributes must be appropriate. Hence the symbolic grapes.

During the fifteenth century more and more of the narrative element had worked its way into Madonnas. This process corresponded to the loosening up of the older iconography and to the general humanizing of religious art. What it led to around 1500, even though the subject of the picture is not narrative, can be seen in the Alba Madonna by Raphael (Pl. 26). For a Renaissance

6

Fig. 3. PETRUS CHRISTUS: The Nativity

7

Italian generation, many members of which were faithless and some even accounted not unlike vipers, the overtness of symbolism and activity was needful. The narrative spirit also called for entertaining additions to the *dramatis personae:* St. John here (Pl. 26), St. Joseph there (Pl. 32), plus salient angels, saints, and other figures, who were increasingly less merely devotional and more actively participant. In view of all these changes, it is worthy of remark that the Alba Virgin still keeps in the pose of her body and head the diagonality of the old Hodegetria. Her book too is traditional. From Annunciations, where it conveniently helped express the idea of unexpected intrusion, the book made its way into Madonnas, there to be first widely popular in Flemish art and then to come, with the mid-fifteenth century artistic invasion, down into Italian art.

Another article of Flemish export in the fifteenth century was the sprawling Babe, such as we have in the Nativity by Petrus Christus (Fig. 3). The type is sometimes credited to Rogier van der Weyden, but before his time it had had a long history, and it had remote antecedents even in Italy (Fig. 4). It does not look the same in the Virgin's arms as it does alone, but in either case it was not exactly to Italian taste. For in Italy even the Bambino Vispo (Frisky Babe) was a self-possessed type. Thus it comes about that in Giovanni Bellini's fifteenth-century Madonna at the National Gallery (Pl. 29) the Babe sprawls indeed, but He sprawls Italian-wise, remotely recalling Ambrogio Lorenzetti's (Fig. 4) despite the unclad display of Renaissance anatomy. The vague reminiscence of some ancient fallen warrior, or other antique, in the pose of Bellini's Babe helps one to see why the Germans call Italian Renaissance art 'Classical art.'

Since the ledge motive, as seen in Bellini (Pl. 29) and Zoppo (Pl. 13), had proved acceptable in Italy, Dürer could use it with all the more assurance in his Italianized Madonna (Pl. 30). But Dürer's Child, though an erect type, oddly lifted up from the ledge, seems very ill at ease, despite obvious Italianization, and much more adapted to awkward sprawling. Further, the Virgin is

Fig. 4. AMBROGIO LORENZETTI: Madonna Enthroned. Vico l'Abate (Florence), Parish Church

ambiguously sandwiched in between the ledge in front of her and the wall behind her.

This awkwardness in space composition could hardly be more emphasized than by turning directly from Dürer's Madonna to the contemporary Small Cowper Madonna by Raphael (Pl. 34). In it the supreme master of space composition eliminates any confusion by seating the Virgin unequivocally on a low wall and putting no ledge in front of her. Raphael was successfully pursuing a central aim of Italian Renaissance endeavor, that of happily reconciling the past with his present. He did not hesitate to repeat the traditional motives of the old Hodegetria-Glykophilousa complex: the Child supported on the Virgin's left arm, her reaching ('pointing') right hand, the turning of the figures toward each other, the Child's embrace. Yet the whole is transformed by the Renaissance anatomy and counterpoise, and above all by Renaissance humanization.

Throughout Christendom Raphael's Madonnas entered so generally into the picture galleries of artists' minds that after his time some stand toward Raphael had to be taken by painters of Madonnas. They could pay tribute to him or they could more or less consciously rebel against him. The former course was taken by the greater number of Italian painters, and by many others, including so thoughtful an artist as Poussin. Despite his seventeenth-century mood and style, it is evident in various pictures how much Poussin keeps of the time-honored Hodegetria, and of

9

Fig. 5. JAN SCOREL: The Rest on the Flight into Egypt

Raphael. The opposite course, of rebellion against Raphael and the Renaissance suavity he stood for, had been taken long before Poussin by the Mannerists of the sixteenth century. For their drastic designs Raphael was no suitable model. The Madonna by Jan Scorel (Fig. 5) is completely anti-Raphaelesque, with its emphatic, agitated drapery scheme and with its Child a pattern of Mannerism, a pattern into which the adjacent tree conveniently falls.

With the Incarnation was connected, besides the Madonna, a vast series of relevant subjects. Salient among these was the Nativity of Christ. As in many of these narrative subjects, the iconography is various and complicated. Right away, for example, in the Nativity, we are confronted with the existence of the canonical account, which gives the setting as a stable, versus the uncanonical, which gives the setting as a cave. That the two were not irreconcilable is a commonplace. Their conflation is shown in the earliest Nativity in the National Gallery, that by Duccio (Pl. 5).

This panel is part of an extensive narrative sequence and therefore was not thought of as isolated, despite the prophets that stand guard at either side. It continues the notion of sequence within itself. In the foreground is the washing of the Babe, so important as expressing His humanity. Then He lies neatly swaddled in the crib. The Virgin, though abed, shows near kinship with the contemporary Hodegetria type.

Closely associated with the Nativity is the Epiphany, or Twelfth Night, which we usually think of as the Adoration of the Magi. The twelve-day interval is as nothing in the time-obliterating joy of the season of God's turning toward us, as the sun turns back northward in its yearly course. In the Angelico-Lippi roundel (Pl. 9) there is even a mild suggestion of Saturnalian activity, in which the eye loses itself as it wanders from the paradisial flowery mead in the hallowed foreground back through the more or less ruinous buildings of Bethlehem to the austere desert landscape with jagged outcroppings of barren rock (expressive of the hostility and harshness of the world), beyond which a glimpse of Jerusalem's skyline appears. The Virgin is she of the Hodegetria, but turned toward the adoring Magi, of course. The Child raises His right hand in the Hodegetria gesture of blessing, but sits on His mother's knee, enthroned as befits one receiving royal homage.

In the Adoration which Botticelli painted a generation later (Pl. 31), the group of the Virgin and Child remains basically the same, though turned more toward us. The similarity of the Child is striking. But the vogue of long-waisted females at Botticelli's time has somewhat transformed the Virgin, with her curiously pendant arms. The more worldly character which we expect in a picture of the late fifteenth century accounts for the omission of any bit of paradise, with gay birds and flowers, from the foreground, and for the introduction of a rather friendly landscape in the background, beyond the traditional ruins. If in Botticelli's mind any town lay far away over the hills, it was Florence, not Jerusalem. The worldliness of it all is corroborated by the insertion of a contemporary portrait, an old man at the right, probably the

Fig. 6. JAN VAN EYCK:
The Annunciation

donor. Not long before, Botticelli had painted a most secular Adoration (now in the Uffizi), in which the principal rôles of Magi and entourage were boldly played by members of the Medici family.

Yet another richly cargoed subject of the Incarnation series is the Annunciation. The outstanding example in the National Gallery is that by Jan van Eyck (Fig. 6). It represents a late stage in the millennial development of the iconography of the subject. Older conceptions of the Virgin as domestic, as going for water, working with the wool, or, at least, being in her house (the last conception was generally retained, as in the beautiful example by Giovanni di Paolo, Fig. 19), have all been discarded. Her holiness is now expressed by using a religious edifice as the setting of the Annunciation. To throw the event back in time, Jan van Eyck chose to paint a Romanesque building, which from his point of view was old architecture. The motive of interrupted reading is used to convey the Virgin's surprise. The richness of detail, calculated to captivate the onlooker, includes murals and windows, figured pavement, furniture and flowers (Pl. 121), and reaches its apogee in the elaborate costume of the sceptred and crowned Archangel Annunciate (Pl. 7).

Lying toward the other extremity of the great field of Marian subjects are the North European drawing (Pl. 6) which was made in preparation for a Death of the Virgin, and the glowing picture by the Master of the St. Lucy Legend (Pl. 21). Painted in the same fifteenth century, the Virgin of this picture is not unlike the one by Jan van Eyck (Fig. 6) in her combination of nobility, of which the rich setting serves as corroboration, and humility, of which the same serves as foil. Between the mundane, seen in the landscape below, and the divine, seen in the Heavenly Throne of the Trinity above, the Virgin is the mediatrix. In contrast to this crystalline clarity of thought and expression, the Apocalyptic vision painted by William Blake (Pl. 22) partakes of the nature of a nightmare, but the nightmare of a genius.

The other emergent aspect of the theme of salvation in Christian art—no less fundamental than the Incarnation—is the Redemption, with the Crucifixion as its central subject. This has been handled in the greatest variety of ways, ranging from the simplest Cross to a vast figure-filled scene. The great Cross, or Rood, which dominated the interior of late mediaeval churches, was regularly painted in Italy with the image of the Crucified Redeemer; and other painted figures commonly decorated the ends of the arms, and often the apron, or panels adjacent to the lower arm. A Virgin and a St. John the Evangelist in the National Gallery (Pl. 3) are from such a richly-painted thirteenth-century Crucifix. Their dimensions indicate that they were apron figures, mourners flanking the shaft of the Cross. The Virgin and St. John thus disposed retained their status in the iconography of the Crucifixion through the Christian centuries. But it was always possible to represent the Crucifixion by the Cross alone, or by the Cross with the Crucified alone. Of this last way there is an example on the gold-and-enamel Burgundian morse (Pl. 8). On it God the Father appears in half-length and reaches out His hands symmetrically to support the Cross at the ends of the crossarm. Between His head and Christ's is the Dove, and thus the Crucifixion is absorbed into a Trinity. Only the angels floating in the clouds round about remain somewhat equivocal: are they mourning at the Crucifixion or singing praises to the Trinity?

Sculpture in the round generally and naturally tends toward a simplified iconography of the Crucifixion, and therefore toward limiting the number of figures present. Wayside Crosses seldom have attendant figures, if they even have the Christ, as the Crucifix does which Gossaert painted in his two-paneled picture of St. Jerome (Pl. 20). On the contrary, paintings and reliefs just as naturally tend to fill out the side spaces of the Crucifixion with figures. Hence the frequency of the two mourners, Mary and John. In the dour Crucifixion by Cossa (Pl. 10), the two are haggard and grimacing in distress. In Perugino's (Pl. 23), they are more youthful and mild, and self-possessed in pensive contemplation. In Grünewald's (Pl. 24), they are inwardly participant in the suffering, intensely dramatic, and passionately wringing their hands in anguish. Here too the introduction of the Magdalen is an intensifying element. Though Grünewald's is the latest in date of these three Crucifixions, its mourning figures seem in some ways the most mediaeval. This is due partly to the fact that these figures are suppressed under their drapery, and partly to Grünewald's stubborn harshness retained from one side of late mediaeval art in Germany, the so-called Gothic realism. The figure of Christ is distinctive in each of these paintings: in Cossa's, severe and insistently anatomized; in Perugino's, bland, remote, and graceful; in Grünewald's, contorted and agonizingly imminent. Cossa's sturdy Cross is set against a gold background, above a masonry tomb in which dry bones appear. Perugino's neat, slender Cross is elevated in a pleasant coastal landscape, with a background view of a river running under a bridge to a harbor, with people and handsome buildings. Grünewald's Cross is thrown together of mismatching timbers, like the support of a scarecrow, and the background is a gloomy, impenetrable landscape dominated by a threatening crag.

Of the many subjects in art drawn from the ministry and miracles of Christ, it is no wonder that none attained to the prominence and significance of the Madonna and of the Crucifixion. Compared with what these two stand for—namely, the

Incarnation and the Redemption—such things as good fishing and bad health seem puny interests. When we see the story of Christ at the Sea of Galilee illustrated by Tintoretto's picture (Pl. 37), it is the painting rather than the profundity of the religious message that impresses us. Rembrandt has plumbed greater depths, indeed, in the Hundred Guilder Print, perhaps the most famous etching in the world (Pl. 40); but it is still a matter of bodily sickness and earthly healing, only analogous to the sickness of the soul and the Redemption of mankind. There are profound analogic implications, too, in El Greco's Christ Cleansing the Temple, but the picture is essentially mundane (Pl. 38).

To another level still, but one that represents the maximum of human attainment, belong all those myriad subjects in art which derive from the lives of the saints. These subjects were usually fostered because the saints were special patrons or protectors of certain people, institutions, or cities, or because the saints were redoubtable adversaries of evils. Thus St. Benedict was the patron saint of Western monasticism and, as such, figures extensively (Pl. 15). St. John the Baptist was a patron saint of Florence, where Midsummer Day, his natal feast, is the great holiday, with appropriate procession, game, and fireworks. Florentine art is replete with subjects dealing with him; one of the more popular was Herod's banquet (Pl. 16).

It was, however, from the Old Testament that Florence drew its most patriotic figure. To the Florentines the youthful David stood for liberty, sometimes even for revolution. Florence without David is unthinkable. Such a grandiose David as Michelangelo's, made for the main government square, can hardly be imagined elsewhere. It is remarkable enough that one of Donatello's Davids (Pl. 18) should have been allowed to come from Florence to America. More violently expressive of the patriotic content of the David theme for the Florentines is the parade shield painted by Castagno (Pl. 17). This has a real spirit of '76 about it. Only in subject is this religious art at all.

If young David, as the slayer of Goliath, had the requisites of a

15

champion for those who favored a republic, St. George, as chivalrous slayer of the dragon and rescuer of the maiden in distress, was an equally suitable champion for those who maintained chivalric feudalism. St. George's range of potential applicability was greater than David's at the Renaissance period, when republics were few, small, and short-lived; and he bore at least, whatever his origin, the designation of saint. As patron saint he was the pattern of knighthood, and such representations of his gallant exploit as that by Raphael (Pl. 28) were international currency.

The content of the St. George legend seems very secular in comparison with that of the legends of godly knights like St. Hubert or St. Eustace (Pl. 27). With both of them the reward of perfect knighthood is spiritual, with him it is physical. It is as if we had illustrated in the contrast the two sides of the Crusades, the longing for holiness and the desire for conquest.

Only time and the imagination of the later Middle Ages transformed the Roman cavalryman St. Martin of Tours into a representative of knighthood. But knight he became, and later on El Greco made him a very secular sort of Spanish grandee taking his afternoon exercise (Pl. 36). In El Greco even the unclad recipient of St. Martin's almsgiving is somewhat aristocratic.

Of the many-sided career of St. Jerome, apart from his formal rôle as one of the great Fathers of the Church, two facets have received especial attention in art: St. Jerome as Scholar and St. Jerome as Ascetic. The latter is well represented by Desiderio's relief (Pl. 19) and Gossaert's altarpiece wings (Pl. 20), while the two facets are combined in Vouet's painting of St. Jerome and the Angel (Fig. 7).

A rather special case is that of St. Sebastian, protector against the plague. It was less the localized St. Sebastian of Rome than a kind of supernatural power against plague that was in the minds of those who invoked him. Because of his association with plague, from the Renaissance onward he had waves of popularity, unhappily all too frequent. The symbolizing of plague by arrows goes back at least as far as Homer. In receiving these arrows the saint

16

Fig. 7. SIMON VOUET: St. Jerome and the Angel

was a sort of scapegoat, like the cushion a child out of sorts punches full of pins. Only a tardy artist like Tanzio da Varallo would confuse the issue by showing the arrows being extracted (Pl. 39); it was on receiving them that the saint's protective rôle depended. But by the seventeenth century many things in older religious art, its material splendor, its workmanlike conscientiousness, its clarity of meaning, and its depth of emotion, were rapidly fading away.

MYTHOLOGY AND ALLEGORY

W HEN a child plays with a doll, it makes believe the doll sleeps, eats, cries, runs, and otherwise repeats the child's own experiences. These experiences, however, are only those which, through repetition or salience, have entered most vividly into the child's thinking. Hence the child is projecting its own mental life into the doll. Also the child can give the doll a name, and frequently a whole sequence of names, each having associations and significances. The adult counterpart of this is seen in mythological and allegorical art.

The adult has a mental life not only quantitatively different from the child's but qualitatively too. He deals largely in abstractions. His 'doll' that sleeps can be sleep itself, Morpheus. The adult's mind is also more rigid—consistent, he calls it—yet he too will allow a change of name and rôle.

For this changing of names and of rôles the 'talking statues' of Rome are excellent examples. One famous mutilated torso is the Pasquino, alias Menelaos and alias Ajax; a statue is Marforio, alias River God; a bust is Madama Lucrezia, alias Isis.

When the adult's 'doll' belongs to mythology and when to allegory is not very clear, partly because of the looseness of language, partly because of the looseness of thinking. Such a big, but scantily beautiful 'doll' as the Liberty in New York Harbor is an allegory to us now; but future ages, finding traces of all the representations of Liberty in our statuary and coinage might say she had been a figure in our mythology. The Furies and Fates of Classical times are a part of their mythology to us, though a modern Fury or Fate would probably be classed as allegory. Even taking mythology and allegory together, the borderlines dividing them from other categories of subjects are very vacillating and indistinct. Giovanni Bellini's Orpheus (Pl. 43) might reasonably be called a landscape; Andrea del Sarto's Charity (Pl. 52), a religious picture. When the ancient Greeks made a figure of Athena, they were engaged in religious art; when we make one, often calling it

Minerva, it belongs to mythology—or, if dubbed Wisdom, becomes allegory.

Venus, at any rate, whatever her status, is a frequent subject in art. Since a cogent and almost universal element of human life is love, which by the adult's habit of abstraction can be dissociated from the particular and become fit for projection, Venus, or something like her, crops up in the art of the most widely differing civilizations. The force of ancient example makes her a favorite in sculpture. Her rôle is various but normally includes being as seductive as possible. This usually involves considerable exposure, or at least the suggestion of what exposure would reveal. Falconet's Venus (Pl. 48) may be taken as illustration. The association with the sea is natural for one who must be freshly bathed. The doves are a transparent reference to love-making. The Cupids are part of a long historical complex firmly domiciled in the Occidental mind and refer *inter alia* to the fruits and motives of love. It happens that this Venus, being Rococo, is so doll-like that removed from her seat, reproduced in plastic, and given less bust and more clothes, she would be at home among the dolls in a nursery, where she too would probably acquire numerous names and rôles.

Tastes differ. And we can hardly imagine that a partisan of Falconet's long-legged creature would find to his taste the Manneristic and voluptuous Venus of Riccio's plaquette (Pl. 41). But the latter has her points too, being obviously mature, healthy, and vivacious. The punishment of Cupid adds a touch of spice.

In painting, Titian's late Renaissance and somewhat mannered picture (Pl. 47) shows the elaborate, but appropriate, toilet of Venus. She corresponds, of course, to the taste of his time and clientele—a bit too heavy for the admirers of Falconet, a bit too phlegmatic for those of Riccio.

It should be noted that, in each of the cases mentioned, the name of Venus is, like the names children give their dolls, good enough but not absolutely necessary. The figure is merely playing the rôle. Let Alfonso d'Este walk into her presence, and Titian's Venus would become Laura de' Dianti. If the unhappy Cupid were replaced with a lion, Riccio's Venus would become Fortitude. As for Falconet's, give her a pair of wings and she would become Psyche, while with a bow and quiver and woodland setting she would become her opposite, Diana. Much of mythological and allegorical art is so equivocal that it tends to become an art of attributes.

Since the Rococo taste of Falconet bore some resemblance to that of Tiepolo, Tiepolo's Daphne (Pl. 50) is of a kind with Falconet's Venus. But here we pass on, as children like to do with their dolls, to the enactment of a story. The story suggests a a motive—hence the Cupid, and a witness—hence the lethargic paternal River God. But full of fire, Apollo comes rushing like some fairy prince not to wake, alas, a sleeping beauty, but to cause his beloved's relapse into dendroid immobility.

The value of such a story in intensifying the projected mental life is clear enough when a picture like Tiepolo's is compared with allegories devoid of narrative—for example, the Allegory of Music by Boucher (Pl. 49). Here the 'dolls,' despite their show of activity, are doing nothing, and there is nothing remotely musical except the instruments and score; in fact, the birds and flowers and clouds tend to obscure the subject. Andrea del Sarto's painting (Pl. 52) is more satisfying as a projection of the idea of Charity, because irrelevancies are not made so conspicuous.

To put drama into the situation, whether with a child's dolls or with allegorical figures, a frequent device is to set up a paired contrast. One of the pair is very good; its fellow is very bad. That is to say, they are Virtue and Vice—an immortal subject in art, which still flourishes vigorously in the twentieth century. Though it may lead to confusion, close kinship of the opposed two, kinship of the Seth-Osiris type, is sometimes used to heighten the tension. The Virtue and Vice by Adriaen de Vries (Pl. 54) provides a standard example of this motive of paired contrasts. The pair might be twins.

Good and bad, if taken in all possible senses and circumstances, would appear to be all-inclusive, and the range open to an artist dealing with them, limitless. In Lotto's discursive Allegory (Pl. 51) a measure of order is introduced by putting the bad on the right (which from the point of view of the picture is the sinister side) and the good opposite. Even the tree, which serves as divisor, is not indifferent: its trunk has gone bad, but a good branch springs off to the left. While Lotto gives us a neat topography of good and bad, in the Death of the Miser by Bosch (Pl. 53) all is confusion, and we are left waiting with bated breath to learn the result of the confrontation, as if it were of Beauty and the Beast.

Suspense and sequence lie at the heart of story-telling, or did until our contemporary critics turned against plot. Bosch understood how to convey the swift suggestion of things gone by and things to come.

Frequently a child assigns its dolls the names and rôles of characters in the literature it knows. Thus they serve tangibly in a sort of assimilative illustration. Manufacturers of dolls have made hay exploiting the characters in currently popular children's stories. Artists working for adults have also profited along similar lines, and have imposed names and rôles on their figures, given them appropriate accompaniment, and assimilatively illustrated the literature popular among their clientele. There is one great point of difference, indeed: for a child, play is the most serious occupation; for an adult, the least serious. Pictures and sculptures cf the loosely illustrative sort, the majority of which have been connected with Classical literature, do not ordinarily burden the adult with the necessity of entering into them very seriously. They usually accord with his holiday mood. They tax the attention little. They lie further from their literary source than do pure illustrations. Therefore they do not demand close agreement with it, but leave room for inventive originality.

The Circe by Dossi (Pl. 44) is, so far as the main figure is concerned, a case like that of the Venuses. She is a projection of the adult conception of the *femme fatale*. But the other things in Dossi's picture make it story-telling, and the connection with the Odyssey makes it a case of assimilative illustration. That it is not pure illustration of the Odyssey is very clear from the absence of swine. Like a doll in a child's stock company, now Cinderella, now Sleeping Beauty, the Circe has been made to play an equivocal rôle. If a connection with Ariosto's Alcina does explain, it does not change the situation. Such combining of different stories is a regular part of children's play in their ingenuous effort to get a synoptic view of the disorder of the world. To be sure, the effort to get this also occupies the adult, but he pursues the quest with desperate ingenuity rather than with hopeful ingenuousness.

Of the same make as Dossi's Circe-Alcina is the female seated behind the figure of Orpheus in Bellini's picture (Pl. 43). Here the scene of Orpheus taming the beasts has another addition in the apocryphal group to the left. This group derives again, no doubt, from some conflation that occurred as the literary fictions hovered lightly in the consciousness. Nearer to pure illustration (though the musical instrument is, as in Bellini's painting, so patently off) is the less imaginative plaque of Peter Vischer (Pl. 42).

That the Laocoön of El Greco (Pl. 46) is assimilative illustration is obvious from the view of Toledo in the background. Presumably there are overtones of meaning intended which lay outside the contemporaneous aesthetic sphere, but they too would only be an evidence of the tendency to combine, which is characteristic of assimilative illustration. More complex still is the case of Bellini's Feast of the Gods (Pl. 45). For here the Ovidian basis is overlaid so variously by other Classical literary reminiscences, and by Venetian lyricism and pictorial mode in figures and landscape, that the uninitiated, without guidance, would not recognize that he is face to face with the Olympians. To do justice to the subject he must be willing to play too.

PORTRAITURE

PORTRAITURE is an art that in the course of history has had its ups and downs. Its great rôle for many centuries in Roman art is in sharp contrast to its minor rôle for many more centuries in the Middle Ages. The isolation of the individual from his ambient, if that be the goal of portraiture, was just what the Middle Ages did not wish. That the sitter was a contemporary or near contemporary made no difference; like a hero of the distant past he was characterized, but not individualized. It is true, the later mediaeval portraits of the Gothic period differ from earlier mediaeval portraits in that they are, though artificial, often so made up from elements of actuality as to be somewhat convincing. Yet in mediaeval portraiture as a whole, man seems always afraid of being himself; while in Roman portraiture he seems always afraid of being someone else.

In the Italian Primitives the Gothic attitude toward portraiture is continued and extended. Whereas formerly it was in the main only the top echelon of temporal and spiritual greatness that was thought worthy of portrait commemoration, now the horizon was gradually lowered. This follows from the growth of a bourgeois class. For with the emergence of this class and of the attendant *sine qua non* of urbanization, a new wealth not exclusively based on church or state appeared. The new commissioners of art, representing the bourgeoisie, were themselves often of the religious life, but most of their money necessarily came from the lay citizens, and not from the feudal, landed class. The new urban industrial and commercial wealth had its effect on art as on everything else.

Humility had hitherto meant self-obliteration. Portraiture had traditionally been an expression of pride, sometimes as moderate as in the Roman family busts, sometimes as immoderate as in the Pharaonic colossi. Now portraiture found a way of taking on an aspect of humility. Diminutive figures of donors kneel in reverence at the base of religious pictures, as in Lippo Memmi's Madonna (Fig. 8).

Fig. 8. LIPPO MEMMI:
Madonna and Child with Donor

Pride was not scotched, of course. On a wall of Siena's Palazzo Pubblico the great captain Guidoriccio is represented proudly enough (Fig. 9), whether the pride be his own or that of Siena in him. By the time of Masaccio, who marks the first stage of really Renaissance Italian painting, donors, too, are full-sized, even in the presence of the Trinity. Pride not only regains its status in portraiture, but even becomes characteristic of Renaissance culture in general.

Italian Renaissance pride nourished portraiture. The fortunate and the successful wished to commemorate themselves, less as people of station than as self-conscious personalities. While the portrait bust had been used by the whole upper class of the Roman Empire, there were reserved for the imperial families alone the abundant coins and occasional medallions. These were richly sown on Italian soil and gave the Italians of the Renaissance most of their visualizations of their ancient ancestry. What more natural than that they too should wish themselves similarly eternized! The *aes aeternum* of ancient writers was illustrated for their Renaissance readers by coins, which mocked at the millennium and more that had elapsed by the time the Italians developed enthusiasm for collecting them. Prominent among the early coin collectors was Petrarch, and how proud modern numismatists should be to trace their direct lineage back to such a source! A sharer of Petrarch's sentiments for Roman

24

antiquity was the leading Italian intellect of the early fifteenth century, Leon Battista Alberti, whose real greatness is perhaps not yet fully appreciated. Alberti's enthusiasm for ancient usage, besides expressing itself in his writings and architecture, also appears in his portrait plaquette (Pl. 56).

An artist who drew most effectively from ancient sources—probably from medallions more than coins—was Pisanello, who is nearly the inventor and absolutely the perfecter of the art of the medal. Among his works at the National Gallery the nuptial medal of Leonello d'Este, dated 1444, is outstanding (Pl. 57). This profile portrait shows, more than Alberti's, a preoccupation with personal features which recalls Roman portraiture. Again, after the lapse of centuries, recurs the willingness or desire to be different and distinctive. These feelings were not universal, of course, for their prerequisite is an uncommon temerity. Even a bold man, the Duke of Milan, whose medal is among those by Pisanello (Fig. 10), is

Fig. 9. SIMONE MARTINI: Guidoriccio da Fogliano. Siena, Palazzo Pubblico

25

Fig. 10–11. PISANELLO: Medals of Filippo Maria Visconti, Duke of Milan, and Domenico Novello Malatesta, Lord of Cesena

said to have felt qualms about the recording of his repulsive features. Pisanello has given something of their coarseness, but probably stayed his hand. No restraint was needed in the case of young Domenico Novello Malatesta. His wonderful profile by Pisanello (Fig. 11) is one of those portraits of which 'men in after times shall sing.' Thus, Gabriele d'Annunzio:

> A youth with tresses beautiful and waving, profile imperial, throat Apolline—a sovran type of elegance and vigor, so perfect that the imagination could not conceive him living save proof against decay and immutable, as in that circle of metal the artist has encased him, immortal:
>
> *Dux equitum praestans Malatesta Novellus Cesenae dominus.*

We are wont to think of the Ghent Altarpiece and other pictures of its time as marking a sort of new beginning in Northern painting. Yet for portraiture some earlier works are very important. The portrait in Sienese painting of the fourteenth century was profile, and it seems likely that the type passed to France via Avignon. There, presumably, Simone Martini painted both Petrarch and Laura in profile, just as he had painted Guidoriccio (Fig. 9) in Italy. At any rate, the Louvre panel of King Jean le Bon, dating about 1360, and therefore the earliest known independent portrait in French or in any other North European panel painting, is in profile. So is the Richard II on the famous Wilton Diptych and, from the beginning of the fifteenth century, the well-known portrait of John the Fearless of Burgundy. The style of the latter recalls that of the manuscript paintings of the Limbourg brothers (Fig. 21), to whom the Franco-Flemish Portrait of a Lady in the National Gallery is very close (Pl. 55).

The profile portrait maintained prestige in France into the first decades of the fifteenth century, when its place was usurped by the approximately three-quarters head. This type of independent portrait seems to have been indigenous in the North. We know of it there soon after the middle of the fourteenth century; and even during the invasion of the profile from Italy, the paintress Marcia is shown using the three-quarters pose in her precocious self-portrait of 1402 in the *Boccace de Philippe le Hardi* (Fig. 12).

Fig. 12. FRANCO-FLEMISH, 1402:
Marcia Painting her Self-Portrait.
From the *Boccace de Philippe le Hardi*. Paris, Bibliothèque Nationale

27

After the first decades of the fifteenth century, independent portraits in pure profile are long unknown in Northern Europe. The Portrait of a Lady (Pl. 55) is thus one of the last of its profile tradition in the North. It is also one of the first panel portraits of a person rather than an office. The significance of this is that while the Middle Ages regarded the exact appearance of an individual unworthy of record except for authentication (as on a coin), or for commemoration (as on a tomb or donation) we have here, as far as we can tell, a picture intended just to perpetuate a specific face—something the Romans would have understood perfectly, but the Middle Ages never.

With the Ghent Altarpiece we are on the main course of portraiture in Northern painting. Van Eyck's three-quarter portraits (Fig. 13) have a mobile liveliness that the statistical profile lacks, and then they achieve more of the verisimilitude which was expected in the North at this time. The demand for verisimilitude stimulated conscientious study of draperies, accessories, interiors, and landscape. The paintings of a donor and his wife by Petrus Christus well illustrate the fruits of this study (Pl. 58).

A bourgeois pride of possession may have had something to do with the elaborate settings of such portraits as these. It may also be that in the North there was still a mediaeval reluctance of the individual to stand out in bald isolation. Whatever the motives, the tradition of the mere bust portrait, or of the head alone, did not carry over from the fourteenth-century Italian profile type into later Northern portraiture to any great extent, for the hands, at least, are usually added. Northern painters, or sitters, wanted them in, no matter how constrained. The characteristic half-length of a Lady by Rogier is freely posed between three-quarters and full-face, and has the hands (Pl. 59).

Rogier had gone to Italy for the jubilee at mid-century, and the Northern influence that spread in his wake is clearly seen in a Florentine portrait at the National Gallery (Pl. 61). The fluid modeling, the slight turn of the face, and the insertion of the hand all reflect Rogier. On the whole, this Northern invasion, in which

Fig. 13. VAN EYCK: Head of Donor.
Detail from the Ghent Altarpiece. Ghent, St. Bavon

Rogier's art was not alone, was more influential in Italy than the Italian invasion of Avignon times had been in the North. And this was largely because of the new vision and the new technique the Northern artistic invasion brought into Italy with it. Ciriaco of Ancona, who witnessed it, tells of Italians learning oil painting from Rogier, whose art he describes as more divine than human.

Though the profile portrait in Italy did not succumb, it often showed the Northern impact, as in the Ginevra Bentivoglio (Pl. 60), where the distant view recalls those delightful slits of landscape down across which we look, through the interstices of Flemish pictures. The International style in a late and progressive

29

phase had been dignified far and wide by Piero della Francesca in Italy with inevitably profile portraits. At Milan the profile became firmly established under the Visconti, and it survived there through the fifteenth century, as we see in the Bianca Maria Sforza (Pl. 65). Elsewhere also, despite Northern influence, the profile portrait continued to be accepted by the ruling families.

Ambitious Tuscan painters were, however, too open-minded to stick stubbornly to profiles. And neither the long currency of the profile in Italy nor the encouragement given by medals smothered the influence of the Northern incursion. In the case of Botticelli, whose conservative side is notoriously apparent, the profile tradition died hard. It is interesting to see in the Giuliano de' Medici (Pl. 62) how he clings to a profile conception of the face, though he turns it slightly toward us and, with seeming reluctance, tacks on the far side of the forehead. But he does not introduce a hand or allow a vista of distant background, though he opens one valve of the door behind.

It is not just in the particular angle that the significance of the three-quarters pose lies. It lies primarily in the implication of mobility. While profile and full-face suggest something conceptual, the diagonal view implies the perceptual. It is dynamic. It implies a turning and therefore both movement and the space in which to move.

This space may be descriptively treated, as by Petrus Christus (Pl. 58); or it may be only theoretical, as in Rogier (Pl. 59). But both artists get their sitters into the space. The typical Renaissance portrait resists flattening, no matter what the view. If in profile or full-face, it achieves at least a sort of relief map. If in three-quarters pose, it aspires to full rounding in circumambient space.

The plasticity of Renaissance portraits—especially those by Florentine artists—is a natural correlate of the vogue of sculptured portraits, behind which lay the mediaeval commemorative effigies, on tombs, particularly. In Tuscany a feeling akin to that of the old Etruscans and Romans reappeared: namely, that it was desirable for the exact effigies of the dead to be ever present among the

Fig. 14. BENEDETTO DA MAIANO:
A Florentine Statesman

living. Thus, concurrent with the rise of humanistic studies, was produced that series of tomb portraits and detached busts which form one of the greatest glories of the Donatello school. The unidentified Florentine Statesman (Fig. 14) is an example. So trenchant is the characterization in such busts that a visit to the Bargello, where many are housed, seems like attending a Florentine party of the fifteenth century.

In female portrait busts it was inevitable that comeliness should be a primary consideration. Hence the individuality of neither sitter nor artist is salient. To be sure, the somewhat isolated style of Laurana does more readily identify the sculptor, but at the cost of missing still further the specific identity of the portrayed (Pl. 79). Italian Renaissance female busts are often a sort of fashion plates, and their genuine artistic merit is attested by their continuing to possess other than historical value after the fashions they show have passed away.

Although there has recently developed a healthy tendency to redress the former exaggeration which presented the Italian Renaissance as irreligious, there can be no doubt of its proclivity to secularization, as illustrated vividly by the custom of portraying

31

contemporaries as the actors in religious scenes (Pl. 31). Something analogous in sculpture is illustrated in the Youthful Baptist by Antonio Rossellino, the portrait of an unknown junior contemporary (Pl. 67). Every age portrays itself in its ideals, at least covertly; the fifteenth-century Florentines did this openly and blatantly.

The passion of the High Renaissance for counterpoise could not fail to complicate the portrait in three-quarters pose. A good illustration of this is the Young Woman by Sebastiano del Piombo, with the head and body turned in opposed directions (Pl. 68). Usually the counterpoise is a little less neck-stretching, and it was felt sufficient to turn the head to an approximately full-face position. Meanwhile, the general trend in independent portrait paintings was to include more and more of the sitter: busts grew to half-lengths (Pl. 73); half-lengths to three-quarter lengths (Pl. 74); three-quarter-lengths to full-lengths. Even the full-length had long been employed, of course, but normally in context: in miniatures, tapestries, storied glass, and altarpieces. In independent portraits from 1500 onward the full-length was felt to be particularly appropriate for chiefs of state; and it played, for a time, some such rôle as the enthroned full-face portraits of monarchs had played in the Middle Ages. Gradually, however, use of the full-length became a way of expressing respect and flattery for both the titled and the untitled, as we know it in the seventeenth century (Pl. 87), and in the eighteenth (Pls. 89, 90) and nineteenth (Pl. 96).

With this general extension downward of the painted portrait in Occidental art, the sculptured portrait can hardly be said to have kept pace—as indeed, on the whole, sculpture does not seem to have run abreast of painting in many other respects during the last four centuries. Half-lengths were ventured in the sixteenth century (Pl. 83); but the sculptors who experimented with them ran the risk of suggesting either a sort of vivisection or of artificiality, as Leone Leoni did in the bronze of Charles V's head perched on the armless upper half of a suit of armor (Fig. 15). These effects were not drawbacks from the point of view of Mannerism then. Nor are

32

Fig. 15. LEONE LEONI:
Emperor Charles V

they drawbacks now, when again like the Mannerists we feel it permissible to make such sacrifices of verisimilitude to the exigencies of design. But to the taste of the intervening centuries, such separation of art from life as Mannerism practiced was repugnant.

It happens that the most startling Mannerist picture in the National Gallery is, among other things, a portrait (Frontispiece). The woman here portrayed by Clouet shows the various features just enumerated: half-length abbreviation and artful adjustment of anatomy to design, including counterpoise, with head turned a little beyond full-face. Yet this picture, though clearly signed and agreeing with the painter's only other signed work known, and made by a master whose famous name was surrounded by a halo so radiant that scores of miscellaneous pictures of his sixteenth century had been hopefully attributed to him—this picture, being genuine and characteristic, was considered practically negligible as recently as the great exhibition of early French pictures at Paris in 1904. Today the verdict is as opposed as the poles.

From the sixteenth century onward there was a general tendency to increase the paraphernalia accompanying a portrait, with a view to indicating the status, associations, and interests of the sitter. Even the bust portrait often reflected this tendency by its specific attention to costume and insignia. The portrait might become practically an interior. While in earlier times the very fact of being portrayed was sufficient guarantee of distinction, now portraiture had become increasingly accessible to lesser folk. Social differences had to be underlined by attributes and surroundings, things exterior to the portrait, in a sense, but not exterior to the portrayed. Earlier there were two conspicuous types of portrait: one, a

33

personality emergent, and commonly devoid or independent of surroundings; the other, a figure merged in the surroundings, as the devotee on an altarpiece or the deceased on a tomb. Henceforward, the portrayed is predominantly an actor, dressed up at least, usually with the attributes appropriate to his particular station in life (Pls. 73, 75), and frequently elaborately staged, especially if in full-length or nearly so (Pls. 85, 86, 87).

The staging becomes so calculated a part of the portrait that the inscenation often comes to reflect no actual habitat of the sitter, but mere stage scenery. Stage sets as we know them got their effective start in the style of Mannerism. Hence their peculiar, nonstructural architecture, their contempt for scale and proportions, their enrichment by crowding, and their waywardness of direction and correlation, which all became traditional.

The stagey architecture seen in Mannerist pictures (Frontispiece) continued to appear, stylistically revamped, in the portraits of pomp and circumstance of the Baroque (Pl. 82) and Rococo (Pl. 89)—even continued into portrait photography. Stagey landscapes, with their clouds and foliage and their improbable architectural features, recall those ornate, but often somewhat cheap, dingy hangings and screens and other 'props' of the studio in which we who were children two generations ago used to feel so out of place when we had our pictures taken.

Such landscapes tenaciously maintained their hold in portraiture (Pls. 89, 90). Boucher, himself a fertile tapestry designer, brought the millefleurs tapestry up to date and wove the flowered and flowerlike Madame Bergeret into it (Pl. 95). Goya was a tapestry designer too. But he was a master of contrasts. In his portrait of the Marquesa de Pontejos, he projected into his tapestry design a portrait (or two, if you will, for the dog is significant) in a quite boldly contrasting mood (Pl. 90). The marquesa's setting is so stagey that one could imagine withdrawing the coulisse of dark middle ground to reveal more of the boards. And one could imagine the boards creaking if Gainsborough's Georgiana (Pl. 89) should disarrange her theatrical pose by taking a step. Would, perhaps, the trap door appear if the carpet on which the Marchesa of Van Dyck (Pl. 82) so confidently rests were rolled away?

Yet the staginess of these portraits is but a symptom of the momentous changes which took place during the sixteenth century. Portraiture is the record of man's attitude toward man. That attitude was transformed by the religious and political changes of the time, by the discovery and exploration of countries unimagined, and especially by the Copernican erasure of the Ptolemaic system, which had so long and comfortingly made the earth and man the center of the Cosmos. Henceforward, man was not the center. All these and many more considerations dwarfed him in his own estimation. He was dissatisfied with the mediaeval synthesis, distrustful of Renaissance aggressiveness. Whatever he put his hand to, there came upon him a thought of evil. In the enthusiasm of the Renaissance he had been comparable to the angels— favorably so, according to the famous passage of Pico della Mirandola. What he had now become comparable to is well illustrated by the portrait cadavers of the royal house of France (Fig. 16). But though man might admit this awful actuality, he could not endure to spend his time in contemplation of its ghastliness. He

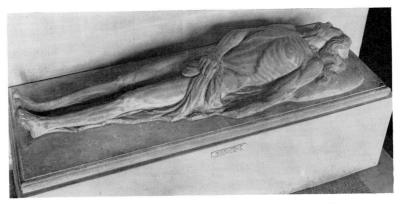

Fig. 16. GIROLAMO DELLA ROBBIA: Effigy of Catherine de'Medici. Paris, Louvre

35

wanted diversion. He wanted support. He wanted escape. All these he found, just as he had in late antiquity (to which the post-Renaissance centuries offer many parallels), in the book.

There is no frigate like a book
To bear one miles away.

On late antique tomb reliefs the reader had become a favorite motive. Now in post-Renaissance portraiture the book again appeared as a conspicuous feature (Pls. 74, 81). The book offered a sort of impersonal distraction, a device to spare the portrayed the necessity of meeting the world face to face. Of course other diversions besides reading could serve the same purpose of intervention: music (Pl. 86) and sport (Pls. 91, 92), for instance. These play the same protective rôle as do children and servants (Pls. 82, 87; Figs. 17, 18), elaborate settings (Pls. 99, 100), and above all, the most favored device man has found for hiding himself in public, festal get-up (Pls. 97, 98).

After the sixteenth century had changed the enthusiasm of the Renaissance into self-questioning, the sitter was rarely presented in such a way as to allow us to feel a direct contact with him. The contrast of the inspiring revelations of Renaissance portraits (Pls. 60, 70) with the varied masking and subterfuges of later portraits is an index of the transformation in man's attitude to man—toward himself and his fellows. When a seventeenth-century artist does unveil the sitter, as in a self-portrait of Rembrandt (Pl. 78), it strikes us as something unusual, and we plunge avidly into an interpretation of the soul of the sitter. When Goya unveils his sitters (Pl. 90), we are astonished that they have not protested, and we begin to busy ourselves with the psyche of Goya.

No opportunity of the sort is ordinarily proffered to us in the common run of Baroque and Rococo portraits, in which we have less of the sitter than of his appurtenances. The lengthening of the portrait from bust and half-length to three-quarters-length and full-length might seem to be a way of telling more of the sitter; actually it proves, like loquacity, to be a shift for telling less. In a

Fig. 17. BRONZINO: A Young Woman and her Little Boy

Renaissance portrait we often feel we are in a direct first-to-second-person relationship; but usually in a Baroque or Rococo portrait the sitter is definitely in the third person. We recall how, throughout most of Europe at this time, the courteous and dignifying form of address shifted away from the second person singular, either to the third person (in German, Spanish, Italian) or to the plural (in French and English); and to tutoyer became vulgar or familiar.

Renaissance portraiture had been a kind of extension of religious painting. The cult of personality it represented was an earthly cult, indeed, but none the less a cult, and with shrines occasionally so named—as the Tempio Malatestiano of Sigismondo Malatesta, and the Pienza of Pius II. Baroque and later portraiture is a kind of extension of genre; it expresses the ambient, the social station, the activities of the sitter. The timelessness of the sitters of the Renaissance (Pl. 59) may profitably be compared with the ephemeral conditioning of those of later times (Pls. 85, 86). Of Napoleon's meteoric career we are given a precisely staged and timed moment, 4:15 A.M. (Pl. 96). Had the picture been painted by some seventeenth-century Dutchman, and were the sitter unidentified, we should without hesitation call it upper-class genre.

The close relationship of portraiture to genre had begun in the period of Mannerism and is fully shown in the picture by Clouet (Frontispiece). It continued through the seventeenth century (Pl. 80), the eighteenth (Pls. 85, 86), and the nineteenth (Pls. 99, 100). Meanwhile the upper-class commissioner—indeed the old upper class itself—had lost ground, and affiliations of portraiture are progressively greater with middle-class and even low-class genre. L'Andalouse of Whistler (Pl. 88) and La Mousmé of Van Gogh (Pl. 102) show respectively these two types of genre in portraiture, and the titles would indicate that the artists were aware of the affiliations.

It might seem that as Mannerism developed and was succeeded by Baroque, portraiture in sculpture, deprived of the half-length, because its truncation was disapproved, and faced with the greater difficulty of the three-quarters-length, would have been constrained to resort to full-length figures. In fact many such full-lengths were made, suitable enough for public monuments. But for private portraiture full-lengths were too cumbrous if life-size and

Fig. 18. FRANÇOIS-HUBERT DROUAIS: Group Portrait

too unimposing if statuettes. Fortunately there was a way out. The portrait bust had the sanction of Classical antiquity: the ancients could not be wrong. By the seventeenth century the bust thus became once more the favored type of private sculptured portrait. The Baroque sculptor à la Bernini might terminate it below as whimsically as he liked with a hurricane of drapery (Pl. 84). Nobody worried about the amputation.

With the rise of Neo-Classicism the portrait bust was assured yet another of its successive crests of popularity, just at the time when independent portraits of children were in vogue. Children had not been unfamiliar in art any more than they were in life. They appear in ancient Egypt, Greece, and Rome. The Christ Child and the Innocents of Bethlehem guaranteed their position throughout Christian art. The Renaissance, under the leadership of Italy, was not disposed to do without them. But to our eyes the modern rôle of children in art seems to be in large part a legacy of the eighteenth century. For then it was that they became an independent theme. Earlier, not only in religious art and mythologies, but in portraiture also, children had ordinarily appeared only in context. Their position in art had been a good deal like what it is in a biographical reference book: they had been there not by virtue of what they themselves were, but because of their family connections. Bronzino's Portrait of a Boy exists because he was his mother's son (Pl. 71; Fig. 17). In a way he is an attribute. Holbein's Edward VI (Pl. 72) was not Edward VI when Holbein painted him. He was a child of Henry VIII. He was very little more than that even as king. Although his portrait occupies an independent panel, and is of a boy that reached the throne, the motive for its painting was not very different from that of the Bronzino boy.

This was not the child life in art that became current in the eighteenth century. The century of Jean-Jacques Rousseau, of the noble savage, of enthusiasm for the *tabula rasa* theory, saw in childhood a rainbow-foot realm where, free from adult evils, the phantasy could play. This realm was a borderland between portraiture and genre. To this borderland belong such pictures as Chardin's House of Cards (Pl. 116), which is genre, but would also be admissible as portraiture, and would unavoidably be so classified if we knew the boy's name. This painting expresses childhood's absorption in its own world; but equally exotic and fascinating to adults is a child looking out upon them from that world of childhood, as we see one doing in the Alexandre Brongniard of Houdon (Pl. 94). Here too we find that genrelike detachment from our adult field of thought which makes eighteenth-century portraits of children so refreshing. How great the contrast with the corresponding busts of the Renaissance (Pls. 67, 93)! For then, when the twin of portraiture was not genre but religious art, the children gave their proxies to the Christ Child and John the Baptist. What could reveal more clearly the essential truth about portraiture in general—that it is neither the sitter nor the artist that it represents, but the precipitate from the commingling of their encounter.

GENRE

RELIGIOUS, mythological, and historical subjects in art involve specific characters and episodes with which we usually have rich associations. Portraiture has to do with personalities, famous or otherwise, but neither anonymous to the portraitist nor frequently intended to be anonymous to us. In contrast, genre is the art of the anonymous. As its name suggests, it is the art dealing with the *genus homo*, in contrast to art dealing with individuals of the genus. Like a scientist's experiments, its validity depends on sticking to what is subject to repetition, on presenting what may happen over and over again, on avoiding the unique example or one-time occurrence.

Among the categories of subject-matter in art, genre may well be as old as any other, but its age has not laden it with honor. It has often and for long periods been looked down upon as something below the salt. So easy is it to confuse the common with the base. Its inherent anonymity and lack of specific associations deprive it of both the name and fame upon which honor largely depends.

Despite this independence of associations, genre subject-matter is anything but lawless and unlimited. It has distinct limitations. For it can include only what has human interest without the prop of overtones of association, without the support of previous acquaintance, and without the advantage of suggesting something through which profit may be had or loss be avoided. Genre is *par excellence* the art of disinterested interest.

Nearly everybody is willing to smile at and make advances to a baby, without having any more knowledge of it than meets the eye. In this banal experience of ours is a good illustration of how genre subjects come about; namely, through the existence of human beings who, like babies, are still of human interest though anonymous and devoid of specific associations. Genre concerns itself with those touches of human nature that make all mankind kin. Infants are among the most widely acceptable of all genre subjects, corresponding as they do to so widespread and inevitable a generic human interest. The Renaissance examples of this subject matter by Verrocchio (Pl. 103) and Peter Vischer (Pl. 104), and the more complicated later example by Clouet (Frontispiece) belong to a central strain in genre.

The generic charm of infancy in art is not to be explained simply by saying that in undifferentiated infancy everyone sees one's self reflected. For the truth is we are all much more like people of our own age, toward whom our attitude is wholly different, and stand-offish. Infancy is, rather, something strange and inaccessible to us. Even our own infancy is foreign and irrecoverable. We know ourselves, as far as we do know ourselves, only from the age of continuous, consistent memory onward. What lay before that, even in our own individual cases, has become an unknown. We automatically recognize this detachment of infancy from us by making strange sounds and assuming unwonted expressions in our effort to establish contact with a baby. It is precisely this detachment, with its concomitant lack of responsibility, that invests infancy with the disinterested interest suitable for a subject of genre. Incapable of escaping feelings of attachment and responsibility, parents could scarcely look upon the portrayal of their own infants as genre.

In many of the animals among which we live with so little mutual understanding on the whole, we see at least a benignity toward all infants of their species and sometimes toward infants of related species. If these animals were to practise art, it might very conceivably include something like our genre dealing with infancy. But most other classes of what we know as genre arise from more distinctively human traits.

An idiosyncrasy of man is insatiable curiosity. This curiosity of ours, being a salient, compulsive, and superpersonal factor of human nature, produces a general human interest in curiosity itself, for man is inevitably interested in himself and his own nature. The psychological situation is clearly revealed in the interest we are inclined to take in spectators and representations of spectators. Just as the excitement of great gatherings at sports events is largely the stimulus of seeing the spectators, or as the interest of first-nighters is largely focused on the other first-nighters, so in pictures that have a subject of some other category, the genre element of anonymous spectators has a great separate attraction. Thus in the tondo of the Adoration of the Magi (Pl. 9) the spectators contribute interesting genre for us (Pl. 106).

Anonymity and loss of themselves in the crowd, with the corollary, the slithering-off of responsibility, make up a great part of the pleasure of release which the shouting thousands feel at a sports event. It is said that millions live in our great cities partly because of some such release. The bystanders in the Adoration seem to possess a similar anonymous and irresponsible status. When a person becomes a spectator of spectators, as he often does in a crowd, and as always before such genre in a picture, it means that for the nonce he 'would rather see than be one.' He is paying tribute to the generic human trait of curiosity and is enjoying the pleasure of self-realization.

There may be a little of this spectator interest about the genre-like shepherds in a Nativity such as that of Petrus Christus (Fig. 3; Pl. 105). But here we are treading uncertain ground, for the shepherds are part of the religious subject.

One of the great pleasures of travel is the feeling of irresponsibility. In foreign surroundings the traveler finds himself present and even occasionally, if he chooses, voluntarily participant in the life of the place he is visiting, without being deeply responsible for its outcome. So too with much genre in art, we look in on it without being intellectually or emotionally involved. If a student of art is looking at genre to learn about the customs and costumes of other places and times, he is merely using art as a tool for social history. For such a purpose the shepherds of Petrus Christus might have some small importance. Their main value, outside their rôle as part of the subject, lies elsewhere. It lies in a detachment from ourselves, like that which favors infancy as a genre subject. Genre deals with people whom we are not.

Genre takes us on a holiday. It has a happy world-approving

44

quality. The world-shunning would not find its subjects worth while. For them there are no holidays, only holy days and commemorations. On genre's holiday excursion we can look in an unfamiliar window and see a sort of Dutch Cinderella painted by Rembrandt (Pl. 113), about whom we can make up our own story without the discomforting paraphernalia of half-sisters, stepmother, tight footwear, or midnight curfew. Or in a blither mood, we can espy at another window (Pl. 115)—to which we might like to imagine ourselves returning in the Spanish moonlight to sing and strum the guitar—ingredients of a romance. Indeed, genre opens up a window on life, but not a door.

We need not be, like Laurence Sterne, exclusively committed to 'a sentimental journey.' For other moods, genre gives us looks at alien people and activity. We may be intrigued by the way a French lady's maid gets water for her mistress' bath (Frontispiece). We may glimpse a Spanish woman sewing and be held intent by her intentness (Pl. 114). Velázquez did not paint her for a Spanish needlewoman to buy and enjoy, but for those to whom she offered a diversion. Or we may see a French kitchen maid in her surroundings (Pl. 117), whom Chardin did not paint for a client of her walk of life. Probably an actual kitchen maid of the time would have judged the picture faulty and complained of some allegedly skimped or omitted detail. Generations after Burns, as before him, to see ourselves as others see us is impossible. Similarly, contemporary shepherds could hardly have seen in Petrus Christus' shepherds (Pl. 105) any of the convincing charm of genre they have for us.

Art is not an interest to be forgotten even on a pleasure tour, and genre has not failed to include glimpses into the studio. The example by Daumier (Pl. 118) seems at first sight almost too serious for the category. But we presently discover that we are not looking at portraits of the famous. Whoever posed, this is generalized from what has happened to what happens often. The chattering flocks of migratory tourists that visit Paris annually are hungry for just such sights as this. But genre is fireside travel, a

45

traveling however that sedulously avoids the lions, and even the guidebook's single asterisks.

Travelers take delight in observing the pleasures and merry-making wherever they go. In this connection they may be superciliously enjoying in part their detachment, but they are also not proof against being infected by the spirit of the occasion. And there is another thing of a more practical character than is usual with genre. Travelers are always on the lookout for new, untasted pleasures. It may be only a poetic truth that melodies 'unheard are sweeter,' but it is a prosaic truth that pleasures untasted are more fascinating. Eagerness to learn of these is not limited to travelers and fanciers of genre.

Merely qua subject de Hooch's Courtyard (Pl. 112) has a triple appeal: the suggestion of alien pleasures, the direct communication of well-being, and the snatch of life offered without any counterclaim. Through familiarity with such a scene the first of these appeals would tend to disappear. The second would be strengthened. The third would remain constant; and it is the basic attraction of genre. In Steen's more boisterous picture, The Dancing Couple (Pl. 108), the artist seems to have consciously counted on the pleasure's being infectious, even at the cost of loss of detachment. Louis Le Nain's Interior (Pl. 109) veers toward the other extreme. With such scant refreshment there is no infection of pleasure at all, and the sombreness of the figures increases the detachment. In Manet's even more cheerless picture, The Old Musician (Pl. 110), only the mute musical instrument remains to suggest entertainment, and we look on as observers of a life that is not ours nor one that we particularly desire.

Besides curiosity, another of the more distinctively human traits is the love of games. This goes back to something that has been more troublesome to man than even his curiosity: namely, to his faculty for indecision. A great deal has been made of the imaginary donkey perishing of hunger between the two ricks of hay because of their being equidistant from him. This donkey is man, not a four-footed beast. As any bird-watcher knows, a bird turns instantly from courting to eating and to fighting or flight without any evidence of an intermediate phase of ambivalence or indecision. Intervals of observation there may be, but they are not essential. So it is regularly with man's animal associates. 'Frets doubt the beast?' would have been enough; the stipulation 'maw-crammed' is superfluous. But man keeps open house in his mind for a number of competing considerations and an inconsistent variety of emotions. This makes games possible. Otherwise, choice in the sense it appears in games would not exist.

Games notoriously offer the biggest exhibition of human nature. They are therefore eminently suitable to the art of genre, the art of human nature. In the Card Players of Lucas van Leyden (Pl. 107) the stakes are high, the players numerous, and the run of the cards a very serious matter. In Chardin's House of Cards (Pl. 116) there is no stake, no company of players, and the run of the cards is apparently indifferent. But in both pictures there is an intentness on what is going on, a complete absorption that proves infectious to us like the intentness of the Spanish Needlewoman of Velázquez (Pl. 114). On the other hand, in Pietro Longhi's Pignatta (Pl. 119) or in Fragonard's Blindman's Buff (Pl. 120) everybody is relaxed, and that is infectious too. But never is it the game itself that matters, rather the underlying humanity, of which we are a part without attendant responsibilities.

The inclusion of Vermeer's domestic interiors as a part of genre painting has been questioned. Is he a landscapist come indoors and painting patterns of light which happen to fall on people, furniture, and walls? Or are these his idea of motives for a more human still-life painting? In any event, he is a genre painter, *a fortiori*, in the remarkable detachment he enforces between us and the quiet actors on his luminous stage. De Hooch (Pl. 112) seems to take as a matter of course our exclusion and detachment from his pleasant groups; Steen (Pl. 108) seems rather to deprecate our not being admitted to his crowds; but Vermeer (Pl. 111) forbids our intrusion into the exquisite world of his self-isolating figures.

47

STILL LIFE

AMONG the principal categories in which art works are classified according to subject, still life shows a peculiar exclusiveness: it is normally confined to painting alone. The very mention of a still life calls up the vision of a painting. Historically, the essence of still life has been color. The further remove from actuality which comparative want of color imposes on graphic arts other than painting makes them of very restricted adequacy for still life.

A still-life architecture might seem as nonsensical as a portrait architecture. Yet in a sense the miniature villages of our fair grounds are the architectural analogue of still life. A much more striking analogue of still life exists in the plastic arts. Toys are still life in the main. Sculpture of the sort we know in public monuments and architectural decoration is normally life-size or larger; and when still-life material is included as accessory, the large scale is likely to give a banal effect, reminding us of the horrors of life-size Victorian fruit baskets in colored pottery. But reduction to miniature size achieves a certain aesthetic distance. This is what we have in the case of toys. They are primarily of interest for their color, shape, texture, and mimic expressiveness. They are intended to provide sensations without heavy burden of ideas, to be handled unpurposively, unlike games, with which they are often unhappily and illogically confused.

These analogues of still-life painting, however timid and remote, throw some light upon its character. They show how still life speaks directly to our senses without intervention of other interests. This disengagement of still life explains in part why it has played so great a rôle in our own times, with their horror of anything anecdotic or literary, and with their implicit theory of 'l'art pour l'art.' It also explains why in centuries gone by still life was regarded as a minor category of art, and was commonly relegated to an ancillary position, as incident to figure composition.

An excellent illustration of this subordinate position of still life is to be seen in Jan van Eyck's Annunciation (Fig. 6; Pl. 121). Other things in the picture, figures, building, even the *prie-dieu* with open book, belong to the religious subject. But the still life of flowers and cushioned stool, while appropriate to the subject, is a kind of bonus, a pure appeal to the senses. The senses have come in for much disparagement in the course of human history. What appeals to them has been deprecated. The pleasures of the senses have been condemned from olden times. As a result, still life has led a kind of underground existence for long periods in the history of art, inextinguishable but inconspicuous, as in the van Eyck. A more striking example of this underground existence is the Chalice of St. John the Evangelist (Pl. 122) hidden away on the back of the St. Veronica by Memling (Pl. 132), and further hidden under its cloak of symbolism.

The subjects of many pictures make ancillary still-life features practically inescapable. The *prie-dieu* and open book were such features in the iconography of the Annunciation in the time of Jan van Eyck. When Bellini painted The Feast of the Gods (Pl. 45) the subject called for something to feast upon—that is, for still life. Just as when trooping through palaces from which their former noble or royal tenants have been ousted, we marvel at the inconveniences, so we may feel some astonishment at the scantiness of the Olympian fare. But both the food and its container are choice, and we trust to the ambrosial nectar to make up for other shortages.

At Bellini's time a Netherlandish painter would ordinarily be inclined to take more interest in still life than his figure-loving Italian contemporaries did. For example, a picture almost contemporary with Bellini's is Lucas van Leyden's Card Players (Pls. 107, 123). In it, quite without reference to requirements of the subject, are inserted separately two of the standard still-life compositions, the cupboard and the table setting.

The sixteenth century grew as prone to examine as the fifteenth had been to admire. Clouet's penetrating gaze is like Holbein's, but each reported in his own idiom. As dispassionate observers, they were by natural bent scientists born before their time; as painters they were practitioners adjusted to their time. Their attitude of scrutiny profited still life. The vessel of fruit resting on a cloth in his 'Diane de Poitiers' has been inspected by Clouet with a Linnaean attentiveness of which his predecessors would have thought it unworthy in such a context (Frontispiece; Pl. 127). Both Holbein and Clouet explored and revealed possibilities in still life without pursuing them.

The intrusion of still-life motives into all classes of painting increases as time goes on. By the seventeenth century we have such notable examples of this trend as The Dancing Couple by Jan Steen (Pl. 108) and A French Interior by Louis Le Nain (Pl. 109).

In the eighteenth century it was natural for the genre painter Chardin to give great attention to still life, especially in a picture like The Kitchen Maid (Pls. 117, 129), where the subject makes a bid for it. But Chardin's interest is far more than dutiful; it is affectionate. More symptomatic, because more unexpected, is the copious obtrusion of still life in the portraits of academic Frenchmen, who were theoretically scornful of it. The Group Portrait by François-Hubert Drouais (Fig. 18) may have become so exaggerated an example of this obtrusion because it was really a conversation piece, but even this would not explain the loving care the painter showed for still life (Pl. 128).

Independent still-life pictures, which gradually became more frequent in the course of the Renaissance period, did not catch on with the Italians as they did elsewhere. At no time can they be said to have attained wide popularity in Italy. There they remained a relative rarity until about the time of Caravaggio, when a few extraordinary examples were painted, of which one in the National Gallery is representative (Pl. 125). It shows the standard composition of a table setting such as we have seen inserted by Lucas van Leyden (Pl. 123). But its profusion and succulency are eloquent of the red-blooded character that created it.

Meanwhile in the North, particularly in Netherlandish painting, still life was rising to the honor of a major category, the ultimate refinement of which in the seventeenth century is well illustrated by Willem Kalf's picture, with its richness of textures and reflections (Pl. 124).

Fortified by the dynamics of the Baroque, which were able to lend aesthetic vitality even to *nature morte*, the independent still lifes of the seventeenth-century painters of the Low Countries achieved a measure of international prestige and found both market and emulation abroad. Illustrative for Spain is the still life dated 1627, of Juan van der Hamen y Leon, a painter of Flemish extraction, born and working in Madrid (Pl. 126). Whatever his picture may owe to Northern tradition, it is unambiguously Spanish, as doubtless young Juan himself was. The stepped ledge composition is a standard one for still life and was already current in Pompeian painting. After its seventeenth-century florescence the conspicuous pictorial possibilities of still life were destined not to be neglected again.

Modern painters have found still life well suited to many of their needs. In their pursuit of the purely aesthetic it has been more tractable than other categories of subject-matter. If artists are not to divorce themselves entirely from subject-matter, as many have done, still life offers the next widest option. That a leader like Cézanne should make much of still life was, given his aims, quite inevitable. His Vase of Flowers (Pl. 130) represents something, indeed, but represents as program music does, not for the sake of the representation but to give birth to a design—whether it be musical or pictorial—in the artist's mind, a design to which what is represented is midwife, as it were.

LANDSCAPE

THE upsurge of landscape in art during the present millennium may be roughly charted in several stages. In most mediaeval Christian art the importance of landscape settings was minimized, and they could readily be lacking in patently out-of-door subjects. When landscape elements were introduced they were meant as indications, as symbolic abstractions, rather than representations, and were treated decoratively. In the Gothic, however, these landscape elements began to be looked upon with more interest for their own sake; and it was the achievement of Gothic's late International phase, which led over to the Renaissance, to organize them into convincing unitary settings. With the unitary setting there naturally awoke a keen consciousness of the smallness of man, and Renaissance artists began sporadically to reduce the scale of figures to surroundings (Pl. 20). Post-Renaissance artists continued this reduction and brought the figures near the vanishing point (Pl. 143). The fledgling landscape finally took flight from the nest of the figure subject, where it had been nurtured.

The index to the rise of landscape clearly lies in the settings of figure subjects. These settings run the whole gamut from no setting to no figure subject. Of no setting a typical example is the painted Crucifix, where the shape of the painting is the shape of the figured object. The locus is quite unindicated. Hence, tremendously effective in its original ecclesiastical environment, the Crucifix looks out of place on a barren museum wall. A counterpart in sculpture is the detached statue. It has been said that the sculptor honors his hero by placing him in a void. This is the opposite of the pure landscape, which honors the setting to the exclusion of the figure.

The gold backgrounds of the Middle Ages are not the denial of space or setting (Pl. 5). They are the assertion of a transcendental setting and infinite space, in contrast to an earthly setting and finite space. To serve the same purpose, of freeing the subject from earthly finiteness, other plain colors were available, notably blue, which became common in Italian frescoes. It is interesting to observe the competition of blue with gold at the end of the Middle Ages. As transcendentalism was waning and efforts to revive it proved abortive, blue had the advantage of its association with the sky, where it long enjoyed an exaggerated use because of its traditional prestige as a background color. Even gold was tenacious until the High Renaissance.

In the later Middle Ages we find the plain gold background more and more frequently overlaid by a textile-like pattern, in case the intention is to convey the notion of an enclosed space. For out-of-door scenes the same enclosing effect was obtained by the use of the verdure background or screen, a primeval inheritance of which a vestige is still to be found in the Expulsion episode of a painting by Giovanni di Paolo (Fig. 19). In both of these cases

Fig. 19. GIOVANNI DI PAOLO: The Annunciation

53

there was influence from the Moslems, whose gardening and textiles came, along with their philosophy, their literary traditions, and their science, into the Christian world.

On the whole, the usual landscape settings of Christian art of the Middle Ages are radically different from those in which Classical antiquity set its figure subjects. In Christian art basic landscape patterns are reminiscent of the arid, river-intersected lands that lie beyond the shores of the Eastern Mediterranean. One of these patterns may be designated as the river-bank landscape. Originally it is something fairly specific. It ordinarily consists of a narrow water stripe in the foreground, out of which rises such a bank of cracked mud as only waterways running through dry lands show, and beyond this, a fertile terrain. Deriving from the Near East, where the contrast is between the desert and the sown, this is the landscape of the sown. The river-bank landscape was much used in Early Christian art—regularly in church mosaics (Fig. 20)—and it well accorded with the purpose of giving transcendental, or heavenly, scenes; for both in verbalization and in visualization the Christians put these beyond the River, in Paradise (Persian garden).

The second basic pattern, corresponding to the desert of these same Near Eastern regions, may be designated as the arid rocky landscape. This pattern, though less specific and uniform, may yet be defined as inhospitable patches of terrain out of which emerge barren rocky outcroppings, with cavernous recesses if needed, but with scanty vegetation. Such a landscape stood for the earthly scene, and as earthly subjects constantly increased their ratio to heavenly subjects, this grew more standard for landscape in Christian art. In Duccio (Pl. 5) and Giotto this rocky landscape is conspicuous, and it remains the genetic explanation of certain landscape features of the High Renaissance, of Leonardo's grottoes, for example, and Michelangelo's barren wastes.

Meanwhile the Middle Ages had mined yet another, and most rewarding vein. Antiquity had devoted some attention in art to the seasonal variations. It saw them largely in terms of the primordial

54

Fig. 20. EARLY CHRISTIAN: The Good Shepherd. Ravenna, Galla Placidia

interest in food. So the Seasons of the Roman catacombs with their successive harvests, of wheat for summer, grapes for autumn, olives for winter, and flowers for spring. Toward the end of the Middle Ages, when the physical world ceased to be theoretically a place of trial and temptation and became, rather, a place of merit, a reflection of the glory of God, the ancient Seasons blossomed out, as did the Labors of the Months (Fig. 21). Here again Moslem contacts may have been partially involved, as they are more definitely in the closely related landscapes of venation.

The Labors and the hunting scenes inevitably called for much landscape setting. They could in theory be reconciled to world renunciation, as reminders of original sin and the pursuits and toils that it brought upon man. They were in practice expressions of world approval, with their suggestion at least, and depiction at best, of the beauties of the world man lives in. Gothic art is full of them and their derivatives, and they have been reflected in the art of landscape ever since. The Labors of the Months do not merely present landscape as the scene of man's activities. They show the

55

Fig. 21. POL DE LIMBOURG: April.
From *Les Très Riches Heures du Duc de Berry*. Chantilly, Musée Condé

dual relationship between man and his environment. On the one hand is opposition: man struggles to master and exploit nature, while she resists and threatens him. On the other hand is co-operation: he cultivates and cares for her; she responds and nurtures him. To the first aspect of this dual relationship corresponds the art that deals with the overwhelming, or, as it used to be called, the sublime, in landscape—sometimes called the landscape of horror or of fantasy. To the other aspect corresponds the mood of pastoral bliss—often called ideal landscape. By the end of the Middle Ages the diversity of man's predicament lay apparent. The veil between him and landscape was lifted and, armed with whatever he could use from the arsenal of the past, he was ready to attack where he would the problems offered by the new conceptions of the world about him and of his rôle in it.

For the artist's conquest of landscape there was a new secret weapon, new in the sense that it was an important adaptation of what was already available, secret in the sense that it was not known to all. This weapon we may call 'landscape at a remove.' To explain this we must go back to first principles.

The raw material of landscape, the hydrospheric realm in which we live, is continuous. The horizontal setting of our paired eyes causes us to see it in horizontal bands. Naturally the first step in the artist's organization of this landscape material was the frieze or band composition, which appears in ancient civilizations in all but endless iteration. Friezes rendered the longitudinal continuity. When they were interlocked vertically to give a sense of continuity latitudinally, the effect was that of seeing the whole terrain from above, whether far or near, and at the same time seeing the objects from the side—that is, tilted with respect to their footing (Pl. 15)— and with the same clarity, and usually the same scale, whether far or near. This mode of presentation is called plunging perspective. It was the treasured bequest of antiquity to the Middle Ages and even later times.

Plunging perspective might be a quite satisfying device if it were just a bird's-eye view, or even a succession of such views. It

57

would then correspond to what we see on an aeroplane trip, or in the archives of an aerial reconnaissance. If man were a bird, instead of the featherless biped of Plato's famous definition, a satisfactory plunging perspective of this sort might have resulted. But man is normally earth-bound, and he visualizes things in the profile view they present on the level. So, in practice, plunging perspective is regularly accompanied by these profiles of things, reconciled *ad hoc* to the bird's-eye view of their setting. Plunging perspective is therefore usually a more or less inconsistent combination.

This inconsistency is especially apparent in the case of religious pictures, where the mediaeval tradition was so strong that the foreground, which told the story, could not be freely tampered with. There the landscape continued to be seen from diagonally above and the figures in general from a lower point of view. So they seem precarious, being, as it were, tipped back against the landscape. But in Northern Europe painters discovered the possibility that the lower point of view could also be used for the incidental landscape at a remove from the figure subject, without offense to the tradition associated with the subject. Hence landscape at a remove: that is to say, beyond or outside the focus of the figure subject—usually background, or more distant landscape.

The landscapes of the famous van Eyck altarpiece at Ghent may profitably be examined as illustrations of this landscape at a remove. The figures of the Adoration of the Lamb are still in vestigial frieze composition (Fig. 22). The landscape slopes up abruptly in plunging perspective. As for the figures, those in the foreground clearly show what the point of view is. They stand vertically, tilted back in reference to their landscape support. In harmony with the subject, the landscape of this panel with its plunging perspective is transcendental, descendent from the fertile river-bank terrain. The landscapes of the flanking wings, however, are not tenanted by anything supermundane (Fig. 23). The plunging perspectives of their foregrounds are therefore earthly landscapes, with the infertile terrain and jagged outcroppings that

Fig. 22–23. V A N E Y C K : The Holy Deacons and the Holy Hermits.
Details from the Ghent Altarpiece. Ghent, St. Bavon

descend from the arid rocky landscape. Thus the lower part of the
landscape across the opened altarpiece is discontinuous. In contrast, the upper part, the landscape at a remove from the figure
subjects, is practically continuous. It is seen horizontally, and both
the aridity and the transcendentalism disappear.

Fully to catalogue the examples and variants of this disparity
between landscapes at a remove from figure subjects, and the

landscapes of figure subjects themselves, would mean to consider most of those pictures of the fifteenth century which contain considerable landscape. Nor would even they be all, for the disparity long lingered.

From what evidence we have at present, it would seem that the breeding ground of landscape at a remove was late Gothic manuscript painting, where small isolated friezes of landscape were a frequent feature, not only for calendars and hunting pictures. These friezes were commonly peopled, and might convey religious themes. Such miniatures being of minor scale and importance could be, like Italian predellas, a field for informal inventiveness and experiment. The landscape at a remove came into being when landscape friezes from the borders of manuscript pages were superposed on pictures bearing the traditional mediaeval landscape patterns. This took place first in larger manuscript paintings. The next crucial step was the transfer of the landscape at a remove to altarpieces and murals. Safely rooted there, its gradual permeation, transformation, and destruction of the old landscape patterns was only a question of time, albeit a long time.

The fourteenth-century painters still got along so nicely with the old traditional patterns of landscape that it was sometimes with considerable reluctance that fifteenth-century artists adopted the new landscapes at a remove. Giovanni di Paolo, for instance, carries on with the transcendental and with the rocky landscape, depending on the subject, deep into the fifteenth century. His Expulsion (Fig. 19) illustrates the one; his Epiphany (Fig. 24), the other. The Nativity by Petrus Christus (Fig. 3) is roughly contemporary, but with how different a landscape! Petrus Christus pays, indeed, his perfunctory respects to tradition, by scattering a few stones and bits of wall about the holy personages; then he takes off over a rolling hillock to an Eyckian landscape at a remove.

However unlikely the Eyckian variety of landscape sometimes appears, if only because it is overly urbanized, there can be no doubt that it had underlying it a foundation of memories presumably fortified by sketches. The identification of old St. Paul's

Fig. 24. GIOVANNI DI PAOLO: The Adoration of the Magi

in the van Eyck now in the Frick Collection seems to be proof of sketches.

The growth of interest in the making of landscape sketches may be inaccurately measured by contrasting Villard de Honnecourt, whose thirteenth-century sketchbook omits landscape, with Dürer, who was such an avid sketcher of landscape before the end of the fifteenth century. In Italy Jacopo Bellini is an important figure. His famous sketchbooks show that he had successfully attacked the problem of tying the whole landscape together. His son Giovanni is acknowledged as the demiurge behind the spectacular development of Venetian landscape.

The Bellini tradition continues in the drawings of Domenico Campagnola (Pl. 139). But for its full bloom we naturally turn to the great master of landscape, Giorgione. The landscape of the National Gallery Nativity is an excellent example of the Venetian lyricism to which this artist has lent the name of the Giorgionesque (Pl. 133).

Giorgionesque landscape—genetically Bellinesque, of course—was a flower, if not of a day, at least of shorter effective duration than a normal lifetime. Like so many other growths of the High

Renaissance period, it was promptly frostbitten by the icy gusts of doctrine. The doctrine involved in this case was that of Mannerist landscape. The whole story is recorded without words in the famous Feast of the Gods (Pl. 45). Bellini painted a picture in which time-honored features appeared: the barren, slightly rocky foreground, with a vestige of the river stripe in the water before it, and the verdure screening of the trees behind—all light and cheerful and lyric. Titian, working over the picture, made the foliage lush and piled up the dramatic crags of Mannerism (Pl. 134). Not that Titian was a simon-pure Mannerist. He was too deeply rooted in the Renaissance to approach the style of an El Greco. But in this picture his mountain landscape, with its flashes of light through riven clouds, is in the best Mannerist tradition. The days of landscape based on the mediaeval traditional patterns plus landscape at a remove derived from sketching were drawing to a close.

Mannerism, the new style that arose in the course of the sixteenth century, represented a clear and conscious repudiation of the Renaissance. It took the path of reform illustrated by Michelangelo and the path of secession illustrated by El Greco. Michelangelo's reform involved the exclusion of the here and now, which had attracted Renaissance artists from Donatello to Titian; but we still consider him as a Renaissance artist. El Greco dealt with the here and now in a new, non-Renaissance way that prevents his being so considered. Michelangelo thus figures in the history of landscape negatively, while El Greco figures positively, as one expressing a new attitude. His views of Toledo show his own contemporary habitat, but all the friendliness of Renaissance landscape is gone. Much Mannerist landscape is strange and sensational. With El Greco it becomes inimical and imminent (Pls. 36, 138).

Other Mannerist painters were less drastic. They were content with landscapes that were only eccentric. The exotic landscape of Scorel is a good case in point (Fig. 5; Pl. 137). Here towering mountains are introduced to impress us, and the lower terrain is filled with strangely improbable architecture and vegetation. A bit of the old barren rockiness of foreground remains.

Renaissance artists, like their mediaeval predecessors, ordinarily did their works to order. With the sixteenth century this situation began to change. The change was slight for sculptors, whose costly material makes most larger works depend on commissions to the present day; but for painters it was important. After the invention of printing, what became true of printed books in contrast to manuscripts—namely, that the work was produced for the market rather than for the commissioner—was standard for prints, which both in books and separately became so important a part of art production. In the sixteenth century this change in marketing extended to pictures as well.

In the greater art markets painters worked extensively for prospective customers. Such customers needed to be impressed to excite their interest, yet they wanted something comparatively standard. It was natural that the landscapists should try to meet these conditions, should try to offer a great deal for the money, and should habituate themselves to quantitative abundance. Hirschvogel's landscape in the National Gallery, although a drawing, is a good exemplification (Pl. 135). It is supplied with well-worn standard features: the foreground river stripe is, with its fish net, even reminiscent of Early Christian mosaic. But the distant peak towering above the town adds to the picturesque impressiveness, and the arbitrary vegetation gives a seductive, and somewhat meretricious, strangeness.

Strangeness had made its dramatic appearance the century before in the works of Bosch, which are all the more strange to us because of our unfamiliarity with the store of folk imagery and diabolism upon which he drew. Yet on the whole, his landscapes are the least strange elements of his repertory, being merely such revision and transformation of post-Eyckian Flemish landscape as was necessary to accord with the subject matter of his pictures. Pieter Bruegel and his many imitators went on with the exploitation of this vein through the sixteenth century (Pl. 136). But

63

Bruegel's landscape stands mainly in its own right and includes the figures rather than being dominated by them. This makes it possible for us usually to think of him as a landscape painter, while we think of Bosch as a figure painter.

Just as there is what seems a less strenuous side to the Renaissance, represented by, let us say, Perugino, so there is what seems a less strenuous side to Mannerism, represented by the Carracci, who are often frontiersmen representing a kind of *detente* between Mannerism and Baroque. The truth is that in both periods this less noisy side was highly creative. What we might call its easiness was art that concealed art. The Carracci were adepts in the mountainous scenery of Mannerism, but their mountains are not awesome, nor their burgeoning trees exotic. In fact, the Landscape by Annibale in the National Gallery (Pl. 141) has a rather friendly though not intimate appearance. The easy and orderly disposition of trees and other elements gives it a soothing dignity, which is united with the Mannerist composition. Naturally it all looks stagey to us, because of the long-continued echo of Italian Mannerist landscape in scene painting.

There is in Italian Mannerist landscape a lack of movement that makes it particularly appropriate as the background for the acting on a stage. It serves as a foil and a framework. Some modern stage decor in which this stability has been replaced by distracting rhythms and unquiet composition has brought out through its very failure the favorable side of what had been decried as the excessive formality of Mannerism. The rigidity of Mannerism, however, provoked a reaction toward flexibility, toward the Baroque, a style dealing with volumes in movement. The confrontation of Carracci's Landscape (Pl. 141) with the Forest Scene of Jacob van Ruisdael (Pl. 143) brings out more clearly than words the antithesis of these two period styles.

It is easy to see that Baroque stylistic propensities were highly applicable to landscape. Baroque preoccupation with recession, for instance, often involving a diagonal view of things, led to mastery of the problem of tying together the various parts of a landscape, far and near. The S. Maria della Febbre of Saenredam shows how well the diagonality serves to conduct the eye of the onlooker (Pl. 157).

As Hirschvogel (Pl. 135) offered his prospective buyers something impressive, Saenredam offered them something unfamiliar. His Roman scene (Pl. 157) or Ruisdael's Waterfall (Pl. 143) took the buyers on comfortable excursions. Another possibility was to make something imaginative and poetic, provided the artist had a clientele who could appreciate literary associations, as Claude had (Pl. 142). In default of that kind of sophisticated customers, it was still possible to poetize and arrive at grandeur by using for the landscape poetic subjects within unliterary experience. Rembrandt's Mill is the arch-example of this (Pl. 147).

In Holland especially, because of the elimination from Dutch social structure of the upper estates, it was safer for the landscapist to paint more truth and less poetry. For the bourgeois will value a portrayal either of himself or of his surroundings. It ministers openly or covertly to his pride. If the portrayal of Dutch landscape scenery was a bit idealized, that did not damage its saleability. In the case of Cuyp there is a very considerable element of selection and studied lighting effect—that is to say, idealization (Pl. 145). But on the whole, it is astonishing how much less the Dutch required this than other people have. The great market for prints which, true to the drawings from which they were made, were direct transcripts of the local scene was unparalleled elsewhere in the seventeenth century. And this must have strengthened the artists' desire and ability to devote themselves to recording the world immediately about them (Pl. 140). Outside Icelandic literature, it is hard to say where we could find so much directness as we find in Dutch seventeenth-century art. But we must remember that even the directness is a transforming agent.

Pride in the free possession of a country which had been won against redoubtable natural and human antagonists, nostalgia for familiar scenes on the part of travelers returning from long sojourns overseas, suppression of religious art, climatic conditions

65

that obscured the more pleasant of nature's vistas much of the time—some or all of these may have contributed to the character and quantity of Dutch landscape during the seventeenth century. A variety of motivating forces would correspond to its range, of which we see the wide angle from truth to poetry by comparing two practically coeval works by the same man (Pls. 140 and 147).

The advent of the Rococo amounts to complaint against the Baroque, but not to its eviction. Such revision as took place in landscape was rather a softening of the older Baroque elements than their replacement. Yet the tendency of the Rococo to deal with the movement of surfaces rather than of volumes had its effect, which is seen clearly by a comparison of Fragonard's Swing (Pl. 149) with Ruisdael's Waterfall (Pl. 143). Everything in Rococo is made as weightless as possible. Fragonard's trees and mountains are no heavier than his clouds. The beauty of Fragonard is the beauty of light-drenched surfaces, the light being used to convey color, shape, and texture, but not volume. It was the lack of weight, the absence of intrusiveness, that made Rococo landscape something suitable for the stage, where its influence on scene painting has continued up to the present.

Fragonard illustrates well the two kinds of artificiality abundantly found in Rococo landscapes: the one, a choice of the least natural features of the garden art of the time; the other, an artificial, studied arrangement of now somewhat emasculated mountainous scenery which echoes that of the earlier landscapists and bears some of the charm of those old associations. Gainsborough's Landscape with a Bridge (Pl. 144) is rich in such associations, with its lonely road, its quaint bridge, and its cottage nestled under an improbable crag. The eighteenth century was fascinated by the contrast between the savage and the civilized. Patrons who were proponents of the French park were candidates for Fragonard's pictures, in which the civilized is dominant. Patrons who fancied the English garden were apt to prefer the imaginary wild of Gainsborough, who was probably discreet in refusing to wander out of his way by undertaking a proffered commission for a picture of Lord Hardwicke's formal park. Charmingly as Gainsborough could sketch and paint cultivated England, he knew the majority of his clientele wanted scenery less domesticated and more chimerical, at least less familiar.

For prosperous Englishmen, and many Continentals, of the eighteenth century the grand tour was standard as actuality, expectation, or memory. Sights connected with it were much in demand as vehicles of pleasant associations. Such pictures as two of Campo S. Zanipolo attest this interest (Pls. 158, 159).

The Dutch artists of the seventeenth century had shown what could be done by recording the local scene. But their example was not conspicuously followed by their immediate successors, whether direct descendants or others. The theory of the grand style was inimical to such direct landscape. When their example did begin to bear good fruit again, it was already late in the eighteenth century. Then English artists—even Gainsborough at times—felt the influence of the Dutch. But it was for Constable to go on from where the Dutch left off. He did this so successfully that we unquestioningly turn to him to see how rural England looked in the early nineteenth century, just as we turn to his contemporary, Jane Austen, to learn how it felt. Wivenhoe Park (Pl. 146), like *Pride and Prejudice*, shows this clarity and directness in setting down what we now accept as essential. But again as with the Dutch, the very directness, and the inevitable selection involved, transforms the transcript into a kind of poesy. Constable's picture is an interesting demonstration of how easily some landscapes fall into friezes, and he has here avoided doing violence to its longitudinal continuity.

Constable's very different and longer-lived contemporary, Turner, was far more an arranger. Much of his many-faceted work is explained by remembering that he was to a great extent an illustrator. He leans heavily on literary and historic associations. Not only are the titles of his pictures significant, but he often supplemented them with verse, including his own. He made, especially in his early years, sketches that are as direct as

Constable's work; but he soon developed an interest in looking backward, which did away with ingenuousness. He was evidently bitten by the bug of the sublime; but being a keen observer, he sought out striking effects in the material of his own sense perception. Through extensive travels and indefatigable observation he built up a repertory of unusual visualizations, probably unequaled. His Keelmen Heaving in Coals by Moonlight (Pl. 148) shows many of the characteristics mentioned—plus the important one of mistiness, which plays so large a rôle in his painting, especially of his later years. This mistiness and the penchant for more or less literary accompaniment were traits he shared unknowingly with Chinese painters. But there was this enormous difference: Turner was an onlooker, not a participant in what he saw. He cultivated acquaintanceship, not friendship. Thus it was Constable, not Turner, who could contribute to the *paysage intime* of the nineteenth century.

The rise of the natural sciences had progressed so far that by the nineteenth century, man felt quite comfortable and at home in his natural surroundings. This feeling was the basis of *paysage intime*. The term is usually applied to the art of landscape based on the normal habitat of the artist. But the mood of intimacy could be imposed on the scenes of his travels, as we see in A View near Volterra by Corot (Pl. 151). It is easy to imagine that the horseback traveler in this picture is the artist himself, so lacking is any suggestion of the alien.

France is the country most associated with *paysage intime*, as the designation itself suggests. But the attitude toward landscape it implies grew more common, and even while the outmoded pursuit of the strange—characteristic of the Rocky-Mountain School— still went on, *paysage intime* was taking hold in America, where it is illustrated by Inness, The Lackawanna Valley (Pl. 152).

Whether of artists or of others, intimate lives tend more or less to seem unique to those who live them, merely because no one can fully know the intimate life of anyone else. It is not only every Englishman that is an island. Our intimate lives we can share at best in fragments, and imperfectly, with the very few who are closest to us. By extending his conception of his intimate life to *paysage intime*, the artist came to feel that his way of seeing landscape had a unique and compelling value. Those close to him might share his way with individual variations. Others might with varying success learn to share. Still others might superficially imitate. But a marked variety in ways of seeing was inevitable. Thus came into being the landscapes *intime* and varied of the group known as Impressionists.

Monet's picture of Madame Monet under the Willows is, therefore, not merely an intimate landscape, but one seen in Monet's way (Pl. 150) and not very differently from the way of those other artists who cleaved to his way of seeing. This is not to discount technical, optical, historical, and other matters; it is merely to recognize that these all became fused in the intimate life of the artist and hence appeared in his landscape. Cézanne, in the same years and country, had a different intimate life and a different way of seeing and recording. Of course, those who have tried to share with or imitate him are legion. His landscapes (Pls. 155, 160), are in many respects the opposite of Monet's, though the genesis of their production is the same. Van Gogh's landscape (Pl. 156) is a convincing illustration of the same circumstances, for all the world knows that his intimate life and his art are closely connected.

Henri Rousseau is clearly not in a class with these artists. In a typical example of his work, The Equatorial Jungle (Pl. 154), we have neither an intimate scene nor an intimate way of seeing it. Along with many another avocational artist, he evidently drew upon prints; like popular music, they are easily transposed. His exotic landscape seems derived from colored lithographs. He has returned to the motive of the verdure screen, an undying motive that had never dropped completely out of sight in Western Art since the days of its popularity at the end of the Middle Ages.

That landscape should become so prominent in nineteenth-century art is not astonishing. For with *paysage intime*, and the Romantic movement in general, man discovered the opportunities the art of landscape offered for the externalization of his intimate life. The rising interest in psychology made this externalization seem more and more desirable. There were other opportunities, such as the problem play and the psychological novel, but none so full-bodied and of such ancient pedigree as landscape painting.

PLATES

THE CHALICE OF ABBOT SUGER
About 1140. French

A REMARKABLE richness befitting the importance of its use in the celebration of the Mass distinguishes this unique chalice. It was recorded between 1145 and 1147 by Suger, head of the Abbey of St. Denis and major figure in the rise of the Gothic. Suger, in his account, seems to have been intent on the rarity of the antique sardonyx bowl that he had acquired. He failed to describe what seems more important to us, the mounting his goldsmiths made for the bowl. It is of silver gilt, overlaid with gold filigree and set with rubies, emeralds, jades, and pearls. Especially fine is the monumental bust of Christ, in one of the repoussé gold medallions that encircle the base.

ENTHRONED MADONNA AND CHILD
XIII Century. Byzantine

H ERE, as in Abbot Suger's chalice, costly materials bespeak a holy and majestic dedication. The background is of gold leaf, and such treasures as lapis lazuli were sacrificed to make the pigment for the gleaming draperies. The monumental, hieratic style was evolved in Eastern Christendom but had become so widespread by the thirteenth century that there is uncertainty as to whether this panel was painted in Constantinople or somewhere in Italy or Sicily.

THE MOURNING MADONNA; ST. JOHN THE EVANGELIST
About 1250. By the Master of the Franciscan Crucifixes (Umbrian)

THESE two figures once flanked the shaft, or possibly terminated the arms, of a large painted Crucifix. The conventional arrangement of the drapery folds, the schematic features, the fixed gaze, and the abstract gold background are characteristic of Byzantine art. But there is a hint of Gothic swaying in the pose of the Evangelist and a suggestion of personal emotion in the drooping heads that weigh heavily on the slender hands.

MADONNA AND CHILD
About 1420. By Gentile da Fabriano (Umbrian)

NEARLY two centuries separate this painting from the panels opposite. Still the gold background persists, but it is incised with the graceful figures of adoring angels, now scarcely visible. A caressing sweetness has come into the faces, and the Mother and Child look at each other with human interest. The rippling folds of drapery are another sign of the new delight in grace and beauty that spread through Europe in the wake of the troubadours. Gentile da Fabriano, who painted as he traveled from city to city, was one of the bearers of the new International style.

THE NATIVITY

1308/11. By Duccio (Sienese)

DUCCIO'S great multiple altarpiece of the Madonna in Majesty is both the last rich flowering of the Byzantine style and the first potent expression of the Gothic spirit in Sienese painting. In this panel from the Majestas altarpiece the iconography is Byzantine. The gold background and glowing colors witness the artist's Byzantine inheritance. So do the strange rocky cave that shelters the stable, and the closely grouped figures attending. But Duccio seems to have caught an echo of the troubadour songs wafted down from beyond the Alps. With no intention, probably, of departing from Byzantine tradition, but inspired by a fresh lyricism, he softened the jagged outlines, rounded the drapery folds, and gave a new grace to the pose of the Virgin, a new gentleness to the homage of the angels, a new tenderness to the rite of the Baby's bath, and even a new animation to the sheep and the watch dog.

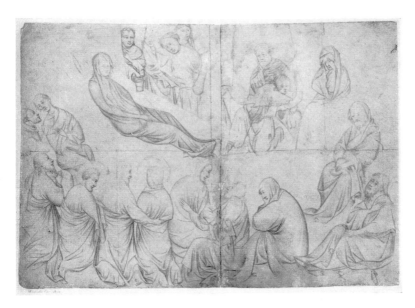

THE DEATH OF THE VIRGIN
About 1390/1400. Franco-Flemish

T HE lyrical grace of which we see an intimation in Duccio is much
more fully realized in this delicate silverpoint drawing. All
Western Europe had by now become so enamored of the rhythmic,
flowing line and gentle, gracious sentiment of the International style
that we cannot be sure where this drawing was made. Possibly it was
done in Paris, where Flemish as well as French artists were active. The
individualized faces may owe something to Flemish interest in realism,
and the courtly grace is perhaps more French. But surely the tender
greeting exchanged between the apostles as they gather from afar for
their last farewell to the Virgin is uniquely expressed by the artist who
made this drawing.

ST. GABRIEL (DETAIL FROM THE ANNUNCIATION, FIG. 6)
About 1425/30. By Jan van Eyck (Flemish)

THE rich materials that seem more symbolic than real in Byzantine painting have come, with van Eyck, into our world of sensibility. There is tactile satisfaction in the cut-velvet cope; and so precise is every detail in this painting that an expert goldsmith could copy in precious metal and jewels the scepter, crown, and brooch. Best of all, the angel smiles, announcing thus his bond with humanity.

MORSE, REPRESENTING THE TRINITY
About 1400. Burgundian (?)

TRAINED as goldsmith as well as painter, Jan van Eyck would have delighted in this intricate piece of ecclesiastical jewelry. It may have been made, indeed, by a contemporary and adoptive compatriot of his. The central group of The Trinity, fashioned of gold and covered with translucent enamel, is so precisely formed that an enlargement gives the effect of monumental sculpture. A similar brooch, or morse, likewise set with six large pearls, fastens the cope worn by van Eyck's Annunciate Angel.

THE ADORATION OF THE MAGI

About 1445. By Fra Angelico and Fra Filippo Lippi (Florentine)

THE Florentine transition from mediaeval spirituality to Renaissance worldliness was hastened by the study of anatomy and perspective and the observation of familiar scenes. The coloring in this painting may seem otherworldly in its blond purity, but the well-rounded forms and individual features have been studied from life. Horses seen from the rear are convincingly foreshortened. The group of bathers is an essay in anatomy (see Pl. 106). And a sense of perspective governs the arrangement of the procession, the spectators in the street, and the servants in the stable. This magnificent tondo has been the pride of its owners, beginning, we believe, with the Medici. For in their inventory made at the death of Lorenzo the Magnificent, in 1492, such a picture appears, with a high valuation.

THE CRUCIFIXION
About 1470/75. By Cossa (Ferrarese)

F ERRARESE artists of the Renaissance looked less than the Florentines at nature and more at sculptured models. Cossa's Christ on
the Cross and the Virgin and St. John seem almost like carved instead of
painted figures. And the gold background, which served in Byzantine
paintings to emphasize the intangible, celestial quality of the subjects,
is here a token of flatness to stress by contrast the substantiality of the
figures. This tondo came from a great altarpiece in Bologna, from which
two other panels have been acquired by the National Gallery of Art.

MADONNA AND CHILD

About 1465. By Agostino di Duccio (Florentine)

As Desiderio da Settignano made reliefs suggestive of painting (see Pl. 19), so Agostino di Duccio made them suggestive of drawing. Here the contours have been sharply cut and the surfaces they enclose kept relatively flat. This technique was essential to Agostino's style; with it he developed a mannered phase of Renaissance sculpture that parallels, more stiffly, the linear sculpture of Athens at the end of the fifth century B.C. The Virgin sits quietly here, but her draperies swirl and flutter. The effect is elegantly decorative, as in some of Botticelli's drawings, and is enhanced by the rich ornament of the niche in the background and the lively pose of the Child.

MADONNA AND CHILD
About 1480. By Carlo Crivelli (Venetian)

L IKE Agostino di Duccio, Crivelli was fascinated by decorative
design. But he got his effect through a retention of Gothic usage
rather than through a modification of Renaissance style. This lovely
half-length Virgin stands in that graceful swaying pose with which
everyone is familiar in statues on Gothic cathedrals; her hands have the
typical mediaeval slenderness and her eyes the long almond shape
inherited from as far back as Byzantine times. For the fruit, which seems
so gratuitously introduced and yet has its symbolical significance,
Crivelli had the example of mediaeval manuscript illumination. And the
gold background is final witness to the artist's nostalgic relation to the
past.

MADONNA AND CHILD
About 1470. By Zoppo (Paduan)

ALTHOUGH he called himself Bolognese in the signature on this painting, Zoppo was trained in Padua. His old master, the antiquarian-minded Squarcione, is said to have traveled far and wide collecting antiquities and plaster casts. Zoppo's profit from studying the collection is proven in these frigidly modeled figures of the Madonna and Child. But though the bodies seem carved from marble and the hair cast in bronze, the types have nothing to do with ancient models. There is a suggestion of Ferrara in the mannered right hand of the Virgin, while her serious face and the reflection of her mood in the Child are worthy of Giovanni Bellini, whose paintings in Venice must have served as a second school for Zoppo.

MADONNA AND CHILD WITH A POMEGRANATE
About 1475. Circle of Verrocchio—possibly Leonardo (Florentine)

FLESH, which suggests marble in the painting by Zoppo, here looks soft and warm; and hair, which is there like bronze, here seems so delicate and silken that a breath would lift it. This tiny painting, only a few inches high, is so nearly unique that critics have long puzzled over its attribution. The exquisite modeling of the flesh, with the most subtle gradation of light and shade, shows already well advanced the development of that *sfumato* (dissolving of one tone into another) which all the world admires in Leonardo's Mona Lisa. The compositional and spiritual relationship between Mother and Child brings the picture close to more than one work associated with Verrocchio. And as for the landscape, which on these two inches of panel stretches into the distance through a luminous atmosphere, we ask, as of the landscape in the Uffizi Baptism, did Verrocchio hold the brush, or was it Leonardo?

ST. BENEDICT ORDERS ST. MAURUS TO THE RESCUE OF
ST. PLACIDUS

About 1445. By Fra Filippo Lippi (Florentine)

MUCH of the pioneering in painting was done in predella panels, small pictures set into the bases of large altarpieces. Subordinate in position and often representing untraditional scenes, these panels offered opportunity for originality and inventiveness that could not be tolerated in formal religious paintings. The beauty-loving Fra Filippo has here experimented with lighting effects. The cinnabar red of the walls and pillars of the cell in which St. Benedict sits is reflected on his face and hands with such faithfulness to nature as we scarcely expect before seventeenth-century Dutch studies of interior light. The scene at the left shows St. Benedict recounting his vision of the drowning Placidus and charging St. Maurus with the rescue. At the right St. Maurus, miraculously borne up on the water, performs his mission.

THE DANCE OF SALOME
1461/62. By Benozzo Gozzoli (Florentine)

THIS recent discovery, another predella panel, is like the preceding in presenting a continuous treatment of subject matter, an age-old type of pictorial narrative that has its classic example in the decoration of the Column of Trajan, at Rome. Gozzoli uses the continuous method in an original way, to carry the eye from side to side and forward and backward, in keeping with the main motive of the picture, the dance. In the right foreground Salome dances before Herod. At the left St. John is beheaded. At the center back Salome presents the head to Herodias.

THE YOUTHFUL DAVID
About 1450. By Castagno (Florentine)

EVEN the Florentine enthusiasm for individual observation was carefully controlled by respect for Classical impersonality and aplomb.
Every detail of this figure and of the landscape background is designed
to express the exciting drama of the slaying of Goliath. But the jagged
rocks, serrated foliage, churned clouds, flying drapery, and serpentine
locks are all strictly stylized, and the sculpturesque form of David seems
fixed in its position, a *symbol* of movement. The picture is painted on
leather stretched over wood, to form a parade shield.

THE DAVID OF THE CASA MARTELLI

About 1435. By Donatello (Florentine)

David, slayer of Goliath and saviour of his people from tyranny, was a favorite subject in liberty-loving Florence. Donatello's version, in contrast to Castagno's, shows the figure in a compact, quiet pose. Yet it is full of potential movement; the inaction seems only momentary. Naturalistic, rather than schematic, in his treatment of detail, Donatello yet caught the spirit of Classical art more fully than did any of his contemporaries. This well-known marble statue takes its name from the Florentine family to whom it belonged until recently. It is already shown about 1535 in a view of the courtyard of the Martelli palace.

ST. JEROME IN THE DESERT
About 1455. By Desiderio da Settignano (Florentine)

WHILE Renaissance painters were striving for sculptural effect (see Pl. 10), sculptors were perfecting pictorial relief. Donatello was one of the pioneers in this development. His pupil Desiderio carried it on. The refinement of such impressionistic relief is nowhere better illustrated than in the figure seen here at the right, running in terror from St. Jerome's lion companion. The delicately modulated surfaces of this figure, with its wind-tossed hair and fluttering robes, suggest a painter's work, just as a sculptor's is suggested by the angular forms of Castagno's David (Pl. 17), which offers in countersense a strikingly parallel pose. To contribute to the pictorial effect of his relief, Desiderio has left round its edge a rim of marble, simulating the frame of a painting.

ST. JEROME PENITENT
About 1512. By Gossaert (Flemish)

LIKE other Northern artists of his time, Gossaert visited Italy, but nothing of the softness and grace of a Desiderio is reflected in this painting. Here every form is hard and sculpturesque. It seems almost possible to hear the pebbles rattle on the rocky ledges. The two panels that form the composition are in monochrome, painted for the outer sides of shutters that once covered the colorful painting of Christ in the Garden, now at Berlin.

MARY, QUEEN OF HEAVEN
About 1485. By the Master of the St. Lucy Legend (Flemish)

LANDSCAPE, brocaded robes, and wind and stringed instruments are as realistic in this painting as the subject is mystical. The Apocalyptic vision of the Woman Clothed with the Sun is merged with themes of the Immaculate Conception and the Assumption, while the setting for the Coronation of the Virgin is prepared at the top of the picture. This combination of mysteries, and the adoring faces lifted toward the Virgin, the gentle hands reaching out to her, the tips of wings touching her head, and the glowing colors of the whole large panel join in the paean of praise, 'Ave Regina Celorum,' inscribed on the sheets of music held by two of the singing angels.

THE WOMAN CLOTHED WITH THE SUN
About 1805/10. By William Blake (British)

R EJOICING in rich, realistic detail, the Master of the St. Lucy
Legend was content to follow traditional iconography. Not so the
visionary poet Blake, who three centuries later painted this original
interpretation of the passage from Revelation. Instead of the pleasant
landscape, here is Apocalyptic chaos; instead of a bevy of adoring
angels, here are heads that float like lost souls in the void; instead of the
rainbow aureole, here the flash of lightning and the Virgin's locks
caught up into darting tongues of fire. Fright, not serene sweetness, is
in her face; for above her is no setting for her coronation, but the 'great
red dragon, having seven heads and ten horns,' the dragon waiting 'to
devour her child as soon as it was born.'

THE CRUCIFIXION (MIDDLE PANEL OF A TRIPTYCH)
About 1485. By Perugino (Umbrian)

THE serenity of these traditional figures, in an equally serene far-reaching landscape, strikes the keynote of Perugino's whole contribution to art. 'Peace I leave with you, my peace I give unto you.' This is the one expression of Christ's mission that the artist presents in each of his religious paintings, whether it represent a smiling Madonna or the dead Christ. It is a message that one understands best in Perugino's native Umbria, a country of soothing distant views, of hills and valleys bathed in a soft, hazy light.

THE SMALL CRUCIFIXION
About 1510. By Grünewald (German)

G RÜNEWALD gave no thought to traditional models. He looked at human tragedy, meditated on the Passion of Our Lord, and painted what he imagined the greatest of all suffering and sorrow to have been. Christ on the Cross is raised only a few inches above the level of the Virgin, St. John, and the Magdalen, who press close to Him, sharing His agony; and the dark, menacing landscape closes in around them. So moving and profound did Grünewald make the scene that we see it as something sublime. The lacerated, contorted body of Christ is transformed into a vision of beauty by the artist's sympathy and the magic of his color and design.

THE REST ON THE FLIGHT INTO EGYPT
About 1510. By Gerard David (Flemish)

'THEY paint in Flanders,' Michelangelo complained, 'only to deceive the eye, things that gladden you . . . without care in selecting or rejecting.' The sunny landscape in which David shows the Holy Family includes just as much of the artist's field of vision as was needed to fill his panel. If he had had more space he would willingly have painted more of the hills and trees. At the bottom of the picture the tips of plants make one wish to push the frame lower, to disclose other flowers and the sparkling stream. The grapes which the Child grasps are indeed symbols of the Passion, but this sad thought is dispelled by the charming eagerness of His whole being, even to the curling toes. Endless details delight the eye. A woven basket, every part of its construction clearly shown, is at the Virgin's feet. Nearby the saddled donkey nibbles at the sparse grass. And farther back Joseph stands awkwardly, in run-down shoes and tucked-up cloak, knocking nuts from a tree.

THE ALBA MADONNA
About 1509. By Raphael (Umbrian)

As surely as David gives a familiar, homely touch to his scene, so inevitably does Raphael lift his subject into the realm of the sublime. Nothing seems accidental or casual here. In this 'perfect composition,' as it is always called where problems of design are discussed, every gesture, every detail is carefully planned in relation to the whole. Not even the smallest accessory could be changed in form or position, and any thought of expanding or contracting the view is intolerable. The Virgin's ample form and broad draperies, her measured movement, and her solemn gaze, reflected in the face of each child, exclude any suggestion of genrelike familiarity. The conscious placing of the plants and flowers, almost ritualistic in precision, emphasizes their symbolic meaning. And the Cross, which might have been a plaything in the hands of the active children, expresses, through the complete concentration of the group, its full portent.

ST. EUSTACE
About 1500. By Dürer (German)

'NATURE has implanted in us the desire of knowing all things,'
Dürer wrote in his fragmentary treatise on art. No work of his,
perhaps, shows more clearly the results of his own search for knowledge
than his engraving of the hunter St. Eustace in wondering adoration of
the Crucifix that appears between the antlers of a stag. With comparable
love and wonder Dürer has drawn the sleek dogs, the endless variety of
plants and trees, the swans reflected in the water, and the castle among
such crags as he saw on his journey to Italy. It is the largest plate he ever
engraved. He signed it with his monogram and gave a print to King
Christian II of Denmark and to other important patrons. Our print is
one of the earliest and finest impressions known, with rich black ink in
the shadows and an amazing sharpness and delicacy of line.

ST. GEORGE AND THE DRAGON
1504/05. By Raphael (Umbrian)

D ÜRER did not meet Raphael in Italy, but Raphael sent some of his drawings to Dürer in exchange for a self-portrait. With what interest they must have looked at each other's art—Dürer's so discursive, so all-inclusive; Raphael's so concentrated and selective! Like Dürer's print of St. Eustace, Raphael's precious little panel of St. George was a gift fit for kings, and before he let it go he set his name in gold letters on the white charger's harness. Around the leg of the knightly saint he bound a blue garter inscribed with the motto of the Order of the Garter: 'Honi soit qui mal y pense.' For the picture was commissioned by Duke Guidobaldo of Urbino as a gift to King Henry VII of England at the time of the duke's election to the English order. The proud list of later owners includes Charles I of England and Catherine the Great of Russia. Each treasured the painting with care, for it has come down to us almost as fresh and flawless as when it left the artist's easel.

MADONNA AND CHILD
About 1480. By Giovanni Bellini (Venetian)

THROUGHOUT his long career Bellini returned over and over again to the simple theme of the Virgin and Child. Here, in an early essay, with the quiet group outlined against a serene Adriatic landscape, he has painted one of the loveliest compositions in his whole series of Madonnas. Though we know little of the history of the painting, the high appreciation of it in the seventeenth century is attested by one of the gallery views painted by David Teniers, showing this Madonna among the pictures in the collection of Archduke Leopold Wilhelm of Austria.

MADONNA AND CHILD
About 1505. By Dürer (German)

PAINTED after Dürer had sojourned in Italy, this picture, with its pyramidal disposition of the Mother supporting her Child on a parapet, bears witness to Dürer's emulation of Bellini, whom he met, and greatly admired, in Venice. But the strained movement of the Child's arms and hands and His intractable locks of hair, which seem charged with electricity, are thoroughly German. The painting was apparently commissioned by the Nuremberg patrician family Haller, whose escutcheon we see in the lower left corner of the panel. Within a few years after the picture was painted, the Strasbourg engraver Wechtlin copied it in a colored woodcut. There it appears set like a jewel in a richly decorated triple frame.

THE ADORATION OF THE MAGI
About 1481/82. By Botticelli (Florentine)

SUCH a master of line as Botticelli could successfully combine in one picture all the movement and detail that is shown here. The restless horses at the edge of the scene prance and strain at their bits; the Magi and their retinue gathered round the Holy Family kneel, bow, gesticulate. Harness is scrolled and festooned, and garments are varied in cut, color, and decoration. Even the background abounds in detail, and its rolling hills and winding roads echo the movement of the foreground. Yet Botticelli has brought all this movement and detail into rhythmic unison. Critics speak of his 'singing line.' Here the keynote is the graceful figure of the little Child, cradled in the circling folds of His Mother's mantle. Toward Him the worshipers sway, like the sweep of the incoming violins in orchestral music.

THE HOLY FAMILY
About 1500. By Giorgione (Venetian)

I F Botticelli's great painting suggests the music of an orchestra, this little masterpiece recalls the note of a distant flute. The idyllic mood that runs like a leitmotif through the work of Bellini (see Pls. 29, 43, and 45) becomes the main theme of his pupil Giorgione. Instead of Botticelli's emphasis on line, here are broad surfaces of rich color; instead of detail and movement, here simplicity and quiet; instead of Roman ruins, here a secluded spot shut off by a homely gate and offering through the arch at the right a distant poetic view of waterfall, cliffs, and houses bathed in evening light.

MADONNA AND CHILD
About 1505. By Carpaccio (Venetian)

IN this, the loveliest of his Madonnas, Carpaccio ranks close to Giorgione as master of the lyric mood (see Pls. 32 and 133). His secret, beyond the magic of his light and color, is a combination of the familiar and the exotic. He conceives a landscape through which the eye never tires of wandering, where shepherds watch their flock and rabbits play; but there are turbaned visitors, too, from far-off lands, and deer with fantastic antlers. Mountains and castles stand close to Venetian canals and bridges as if they belonged there. This plausible juxtaposition of unlikely company is the essence of dreams. And so wrapped in reverie are the Virgin and Child that, though Christ raises His hand in blessing, they do not see beyond the parapet which closes them off in the land of dreams.

THE SMALL COWPER MADONNA
About 1505. By Raphael (Umbrian)

WITH Raphael, the great master of space composition, all is as open and reasonable as the wide vistas of his native Umbria before which he places his figures. Though the Virgin is only partly shown and without the usual limiting parapet in front, the space she and her Child occupy is clearly defined. There is balance and harmony of parts throughout the composition no less than in the typical face of the Virgin, with which Raphael set the norm of beauty that still prevails and makes the purist judge a little harshly the wide mouth and blunt nose of Carpaccio's dreamy Madonna.

MADONNA AND CHILD IN A GARDEN
About 1460. By Tura (Ferrarese)

PERHAPS German influence in Northern Italy may account for some of the imaginative, fantastic tendencies of Ferrarese painting. But Classical teachings in near-by Padua had a steadying influence, and in this painting by Tura the figures are solidly formed in spite of the fanciful detail. The endlessly crinkled drapery, the orange trees bending in adoration toward the foliated aureole, the zigzags and pendent tubes of the Virgin's headdress—all these fantastic details are organized into a strictly mannered pattern. Equally fantastic and equally mannered are the petal-like shape of the Virgin's eyelids, the nervous articulation of her long fingers, and the cradling of the Child between her knees. So consistently unreal is the detail that we accept it as a commentary on the mystery of the Christian theme.

ST. MARTIN AND THE BEGGAR
1597/99. By El Greco (Spanish)

E L GRECO, greatest of Mannerists, refashions visible things according
to the fanciful pattern of his imagination. In this picture we see no
such solidly formed figures as Tura painted. Here the bodies fall into a
rhythmic pattern of elongated luminous shapes. This is El Greco's way
of expressing vital essences, whether human or divine, and corresponds
to his way of giving a kind of life to even the inanimate. Colors seem to
live in this picture, the blue of the sky, the green of the mantle; and one
understands black as never before, in this harness patterned against the
white body of St. Martin's horse.

CHRIST AT THE SEA OF GALILEE
About 1560. By Tintoretto (Venetian)

THE young El Greco had probably not yet come to Venice from Crete when Tintoretto painted this epoch-making picture, one of the most remarkable of early seascapes. But it anticipates the dramatic visions of nature painted by El Greco in his maturity (Pl. 138). The incisive patterns of water and clouds, the striking poses of the seven small figures in the boat, and the forceful contrasts of light and shade are all characteristic of the Mannerist style. Characteristic too is the slender, commanding figure of Christ; and here we see that at its best Mannerism could be reminiscent of Byzantine canons. The scene represented follows faithfully the early verses of John xxi.

CHRIST CLEANSING THE TEMPLE
About 1570. By El Greco (Spanish)

TINTORETTO, Veronese, Titian—even Raphael and Michelangelo—
come in for a share of tribute in this youthful work of El Greco. It
must have been painted soon after he came to Venice to study, and it is
his earliest signed picture. In the meticulously inscribed letters of the
signature, critics see evidence of Byzantine training, perhaps in the
studio of some icon painter in El Greco's native island. *Cretan* he writes
after his name. Yet, in his first ecstasy of enthusiasm for the great
wealth of Italian art, he borrows with feverish haste figures and poses,
costumes and colors. In spite of these miscellaneous borrowings he
builds up a unified composition, the thrusts and counterthrusts of
which are to become characteristic of his brilliant Mannerist style.
Passages in Matthew xxi and Mark xi are interpreted literally by El
Greco in the painting.

ST. SEBASTIAN
About 1625. By Tanzio da Varallo (North Italian)

IN this intricate but splendidly composed painting we have a paragon of the Baroque. This is the style of decoration that was lavished upon churches in Catholic countries throughout the seventeenth century. Reacting against the restraint imposed by the Reformation, the Catholics covered the walls, domes, and altars of their places of worship with painted and carved figures in complicated movement. And whether the scene be one of joy or of martyrdom, a palpitating ecstasy bears witness to its divine significance.

CHRIST HEALING THE SICK
(DETAIL FROM THE HUNDRED GUILDER PRINT)
About 1650. By Rembrandt (Dutch)

REMBRANDT would not have been a successful church decorator in a Catholic country. In his conception of Christianity there was no place for ecstasy. Sympathetic understanding and infinite compassion were his whole theme, whether the subject was a story from the Gospels or merely the features of an old man. But his dramatic use of color relates him to the Baroque period, in which he lived. And we may speak of color even in his etchings, at least in so fine an impression as this one, with its velvety blacks, shading into white.

VENUS CHASTISING CUPID
About 1520. By Riccio (Paduan)

PLAQUETTES were chiefly an outgrowth of the Renaissance interest in the myths of antiquity, as portrait medals were developed to satisfy the Renaissance craving for a personal fame like that of the ancients (see Pl. 57 and Figs. 10, 11). Small, relatively cheap, turned out in a number of castings, usually in bronze, plaquettes could be collected like engravings. Collectors now vie with each other in obtaining the best examples, those most perfectly cast and preserved, from the finest designs of the most important sculptors. Renaissance collectors, usually amateur humanists, were concerned with the subjects, caring little about originality of composition. Even so competent an artist as Riccio did not hesitate to borrow designs. Mantegna's Judith suggested the pose of this Venus, except for the upraised arm, which recalls Giorgione's Venus, as does the beautiful modeling of the body, which makes this one of the finest of Italian plaquettes.

ORPHEUS AND EURYDICE

Probably 1519. By Peter Vischer the Younger (German)

PETER Vischer is believed to have visited Northern Italy. In any case, he introduced its flourishing art of the plaquette into Germany. But he found his models at home, in Nuremberg. His composition of Orpheus and Eurydice is adapted from Dürer's famous engraving of Adam and Eve. The lyric mood, too, is German, less reserved and dreamlike than the lyricism of Venetian art. The pair look at each other with longing and a premonition of their impending fate. Even Eurydice's fluttering drapery and hair, as decorative as corresponding details in Riccio's plaquette, reach out toward the mate whom she will never overtake. No other casting of this plaquette is known; it remains a unique masterpiece, the prince of plaquettes, on which the artist proudly put his stamp, two fish transfixed by a spear.

ORPHEUS

About 1515. By Giovanni Bellini (Venetian)

CLASSICAL mythology furnished many a subject to Renaissance literature and art. But poet and artist refashioned as freely as they borrowed. In this painting, for example, the combination of allusions to ancient literary sources baffles the modern iconographer. Did the Renaissance humanist see here, perhaps, the influence of sorcery as compared with the influence of music and the representative arts? Circe with her magic transforms men into animals; Orpheus with his music holds all nature spellbound; and can it be that the object held by Pan is not white wool, as some have interpreted it, but a sculptured mask, with which he captivates the human mind? Regardless of subject, the charm of the painting lies in its lyric mood, that poetic, dreamlike suspense born, we may imagine, of the mist over the Venetian lagoons. The presence of gazelles among the animals in the wooded background leads us, by a fascinating chain of documents involving menageries and art commissions, to the probable first owner of the picture, Giovanni Cornaro, translator of Artemidoros' *Interpretation of Dreams*.

CIRCE AND HER LOVERS IN A LANDSCAPE
About 1515. By Dosso Dossi (Ferrarese)

W E might be puzzled by Dosso Dossi's refashioning of the Circe myth, as we are by Bellini's, did we not have an explanation in Ariosto's *Orlando Furioso*, written for the same Duke of Ferrara whom Dosso and Bellini served. This poem figures Alcina, Ariosto's variant of Circe. She transforms men into all kinds of animals and birds, employing, instead of the Classical wand, a variety of implements, here a tablet and a book of symbols. The beautiful sorceress might almost be Bellini's Circe in reverse, only more fully developed, for the younger artist looks forward to the more sumptuous High Renaissance, now being ushered in by Titian.

45

THE FEAST OF THE GODS
Dated 1514. By Giovanni Bellini (Venetian)

I N this dream of antiquity Bellini has caught the Arcadian tranquility
which we like to associate with ages remote and poetic to us. These
abstracted figures also have more than a touch of that Greek aloofness
we admire in the Venus de Milo. A lifelong painter of Madonnas and
saints, the octogenarian Bellini brings to an unaccustomed subject his
habitual spirit of reverence. The theme is taken from Ovid's explanation
of the origin of a pagan ritual in honor of Priapus. The untimely braying
of the ass betrays the God of Fertility as he approaches the sleeping
Goddess of Chastity, Vesta. Her comrade deities, drowsed with wine,
have failed to warn her. Thus the ass alone thwarts the will of Priapus
and is doomed to become the sacrificial victim in the ritual. Another
painter has made some surely unsanctioned changes in Bellini's
ceremonial figures. But still the golden-haired nymphs come bearing
their ambrosial bowls with the dignity of Magi in an Epiphany. Titian
repainted the background at the left, giving us his magnificent mountain
view of Cadore (Pl. 134), but disturbing the Classical tranquility of
Bellini's continuous frieze of trees against a sunset sky.

LAOCOÖN

About 1610. By El Greco (Spanish)

E L Greco was yet less concerned than Bellini with pagan lore and
conceded less to it in style. This is his only known mythological
painting. For an ancient parallel one would not think, as in Bellini's case,
of the tranquil Venus de Milo; rather, of the Pergamon Altar, with its
writhing figures. Even the famous ancient Laocoön group, which El
Greco must have seen in Rome, is formal and schematic compared to El
Greco's painting. Instead of forming a compact group, these figures fall
away from each other. Their elongated bodies, arms, and legs reach out
in all directions to stress the vastness of surrounding space. The
dramatic mood also seems expansive. It carries over from the scene in
the foreground to the distant view of Toledo under threatening clouds.
The face of the aged priest of Apollo here reflects the poignant futility
of unwelcome prophecy. The three figures at the right, usually interpreted as deities, betray no awareness of the tragic destruction of
Laocoön and his sons. They are counterparts of the saints who flank
many a Crucifixion uninvolved in its drama. And the Trojan horse,
approaching the city gates, is not merely a pagan motive. It is a symbol,
too, of the doom which El Greco's Toledo was seeking to escape through
religious extravagance—through the consuming flames of the auto-da-fé.

VENUS WITH A MIRROR
About 1555. By Titian (Venetian)

No painting expresses better than this resplendent Venus the ideal of maturity, of full summer ripeness, characteristic of the Venetian Renaissance. The consciousness and pride of self are expressed in ample forms and measured gestures. In the pose of this Venus, which derives from the Classical Venus Pudica, there is no suggestion of shame or modesty. Such concepts are earthly and have no place in the realm of the goddess. Fully aware of the beauty which is hers by divine right, Venus receives the myrtle wreath as unaffectedly as a queen receives her crown. And the little cupids, who bring the wreath and hold the mirror, symbols of the goddess of beauty, are as serious and devoted in their offices as the participants in a religious rite. Titian here pays his tribute to physical beauty, unsullied in its godlike state.

VENUS OF THE DOVES
About 1760. By Falconet (French)

INSTEAD of Titian's monumentality, Falconet gives us Rococo daintiness and soft sensuality. While the jewels entwined in the golden hair of Titian's Venus declare a birthright rather than a passing fashion, the petite head of Falconet's goddess, traditionally identified as Madame de Pompadour, exhibits the art of the court coiffeur. Instead of sumptuous drapery, here are soft, clinging folds which reveal the body, and that body has the svelte grace of a bathing beauty. Even the attendant cupids have become coy and clinging. Titian's Venus calls for the stateliness of a large canvas and sonorous colors; Falconet's requires the intimacy of small proportions and would admit the milky white of porcelain. It was customary for sculptors of the day to furnish designs for the Royal Porcelain Manufactory of Sèvres, and we should not be surprised to find reproductions of this marble group in Sèvres ware, charming *bibelots* for the decoration of drawing rooms.

ALLEGORY OF MUSIC
Dated 1764. By Boucher (French)

THE idealized types and pastel colors of Boucher's seductive mythological and allegorical figures, and the ethereal settings in which he painted them, render delightfully decorative and respectably aloof what might otherwise be indiscreetly sensuous. With doves and cupids, as in Falconet's marble group (Pl. 48), this Allegory of Music is a calculated reminiscence of the pleasant theme of Venus, goddess of love and beauty. Around the relaxed and quiet figure of the muse the playful movement of her attendants is like a circling summer breeze.

APOLLO PURSUING DAPHNE
About 1765. By Tiepolo (Venetian)

T URNING from Boucher's Allegory to this painting by Tiepolo we are
startled as by a flash of lightning. As if to rouse painting from the
lethargy that threatened Italian art after its great past, Tiepolo brought
vigor and movement, fresh glowing color and haughty pride of bearing.
Both he and Boucher carried out vast decorative projects, Boucher with
more suavity and grace, Tiepolo with greater inventiveness and *élan*. It
was apparently in connection with his decorations in the Royal Palace at
Madrid that Tiepolo painted this brilliant study of the metamorphosis
of Daphne at the approach of the shining sun god.

51

ALLEGORY
Dated 1505. By Lotto (Venetian)

THIS painting presents the most imaginative, probably, of all inter-
pretations of a favorite Renaissance allegory, the triumph of Virtue
over Vice. For Vice, there is the wine-guzzling satyr, who reclines in a
flowering woodland, while his doom is foretold beyond in the stormy
sky and sea, with foundering ship. For Virtue, there is the eager child,
gathering up emblems of cultural pursuits from stony ground, while his
triumph is promised in the glowing sky and placid water and by the
tiny many-winged soul climbing swiftly toward a mountain peak above
the clouds. On the side of Virtue, beneath the Medusa shield of the
Goddess of Wisdom, is the coat of arms of Cardinal Bernardo Rossi. For
this enchanting painting, where opposites in symbolism and opposites in
landscape mood are subtly combined, was the cover for Rossi's portrait,
now in Naples. With this allegory the cardinal announced his choice of
the virtuous life.

CHARITY

Probably 1530. By Andrea del Sarto (Florentine)

CHARITY'S rank as the greatest of the theological virtues may be enough to explain its frequent representation in Renaissance art. The subject has the further advantage of approaching iconographically the most beloved of all Christian themes, the Madonna and Child. Lotto might have interpreted the allegory in a more original way. Andrea del Sarto has merely followed the usual personification of Charity as a mother, or nurse, with children clustered round her, the smallest at her breast, like a Christ Child, the others resembling a little St. John, or angels. We must not look for Lotto's subtle inventiveness or for Venetian treatment of landscape. Andrea has given us Florentine excellence of modeling, figure types which are beautiful, yet reserved, and a composition which is mannered in detail, yet noble. We can understand why Niccolò Antinori, who bought the picture soon after Andrea's death, treasured it 'as the rare thing that it truly is.'

THE Triumph of Vice over Virtue is a title one might be tempted to give this allegory. For the knightly accoutrements lie abandoned on the ground, and the tottering old man's rosary is neglected for financial dealings with the devil. But there is still hope of salvation. As Death enters the door, the sinner, abed, hesitates between a bag of gold and the Crucified Christ. With the Northern penchant for the fantastic, Bosch sees Vice as loathsome imps, with frog bodies, rat tails, pig snouts, bat wings. No one could miss the moral of this painting, which is like a caricature in its emphasis. But what one may miss, unless alert to aesthetic overtones, is the translucent sheen in the highlights, the harmony of the subdued colors, and the intentness of mood, which render beautiful and moving what from another hand might have been merely amusing or satirical.

DEATH AND THE MISER
About 1490. By Bosch (Flemish)

VIRTUE AND VICE
Dated 1610. By Adriaen de Vries (Dutch)

WITH the post-Renaissance awareness of the complexity of man, and with the consequent interest in psychological problems, such concepts as virtue and vice had to be reinterpreted. Artists no longer thought in terms of Bosch's fantastically contrived imps or Lotto's mythological satyr (Pl. 51). Virtue and vice were now seen as two natures struggling in man, both clothed with his body. Adriaen de Vries, trained in Italy, though of Northern birth, personifies virtue and vice in Michelangelesque figures, beautiful of feature and strong of body. Only through sheer will, we feel, has Virtue been able to crush underfoot her equally attractive and equally muscular twin sister, Vice. The balanced *contrapposto* of the victorious figure and the writhing movement of the other offer a plastic commentary on the transition of styles, from Mannerism to Baroque.

PORTRAIT OF A LADY
About 1410. Franco-Flemish (Pol de Limbourg ?)

INDEPENDENT portraits are rare at the beginning of the fifteenth century, and we find no close analogue to this one. The scroll-like shaping of features and the enamel-like surface discredit the former attribution to Pisanello. But if we imagine the portrait reduced to miniature size, we are struck by its similarity to the elegant ladies that Pol de Limbourg painted in one of the most marvelous of all illuminated books, 'Les Très Riches Heures du Duc de Berry' (Fig. 21). We should like to identify our sitter with one of the duke's two daughters, of whom documents give us fascinating glimpses. In any case, the portrait presents that combination of individuality and convention that delights us in all the miniatures of the book, in one of which the duke himself is seen sitting at dinner, among his courtiers.

SELF-PORTRAIT
About 1435. By Alberti (Florentine)

THIS plaquette would seem to be a by-product of the humanistic interests which bore fruit in the typical Renaissance medal (see Pl. 57 and Figs. 10, 11). For on a single surface it combines the essentials of a medal's obverse and reverse: portrait and impresa. What more fitting than the winged eye as personal device for this 'universal man,' whose whole life was devoted to physical and mental observation! The inscription gives us his name: Leon Battista Alberti. And that he was the sculptor as well as sitter is a matter of general acceptance. Alberti was not a professional sculptor. Beside the Portrait of a Lady executed by a master craftsman like Pol de Limbourg, this work seems experimental, even amateurish, yet redolent of genius.

MEDAL OF LEONELLO D'ESTE
Dated 1444. By Pisanello (Veronese)

A TYPE of Renaissance portraiture came into vogue through medals, which were in turn patterned on ancient Imperial coins and medallions. Lords of the Italian principalities made collections of ancient coins, and about 1438 Pisanello began adapting the coin type of composition to the larger surfaces of medals, which were usually cast in bronze. In 1446 Flavio Biondo wrote to Leonello d'Este, Lord of Ferrara, congratulating him on having followed the Roman Imperial fashion of using 'coins' for perpetuating features and name. Undoubtedly it was a medal to which Biondo referred, perhaps the one here illustrated, commemorating the marriage of Leonello to Maria, the daughter of Alphonso V of Aragon. For balanced design, clean-cut outline, and delicate relief modeling, as well as for forceful interpretation of character, this medal is unexcelled. The profile view, invariably chosen for portraits by Pisanello, emphasizes the distinctive features and gives an impression of aloofness and permanence. The literal meaning of Leonello's name (little lion) gave the artist an opportunity to use one of his superb animal studies on the reverse of the medal. Here a lion is being taught by Cupid to sing—an original and appropriate allusion to the marriage—while the Este eagle perches on a branch. An impresa of Leonello's, a rigid mast with tugging sail, may be a reference to stability of character.

A DONOR AND HIS WIFE

About 1455. By Petrus Christus (Flemish)

A T the same time that the art of portraiture was being practised in Italy in emulation of antiquity, it was developing in Flanders as an inevitable phase of the naturalism of Jan van Eyck and his circle. Hence the choice of a three-quarters view instead of the profile, the search for momentary effect rather than one of permanence and unchangeableness. With their unprejudiced delight in all creation, Flemish artists not only painted independent portraits of men and women, but included them without apology in devotional pictures. These two donors are probably equal in size to the now lost sacred figures they once flanked, and though we can no longer decipher their coats of arms, they hung them on the wall with perfect self-assurance.

PORTRAIT OF A LADY
About 1455. By Rogier van der Weyden (Flemish)

THE folded hands and lowered eyes of the lady in this painting betray a timidity in freeing portraiture from religious art. But the living presence of the young woman is expressed with such remarkable vividness as to give the impression that she might at any moment raise her eyes and turn her head with a smile. So beautiful is the modeling of the head and throat, enhanced by the transparent veil of sheerest linen, and so sensitive is the arrangement of the hands in front of the elegant red belt that one accepts without question the stylized curves of eyelids and lips and the impossibly small proportions of the hands.

GINEVRA BENTIVOGLIO
About 1480. By Ercole Roberti (Ferrarese)

THE profile of this portrait, one of a pair in the National Gallery, is as precise as the profile on the medal of Leonello d'Este (Pl. 57). But the direct inspiration for the pair was the famous Uffizi diptych of Ginevra's sister and brother-in-law, the Duke and Duchess of Urbino, painted by Piero della Francesca in 1465. The four portraits are of comparable excellence, but while a vast Umbrian landscape spreads out beyond the Uffizi profiles, dark curtains behind Ginevra and her husband leave only a glimpse of their many-towered Bologna. The portrait of Ginevra is entirely secular in conception, yet it does not suggest the lively presence of the sitter that we feel in van der Weyden's work. The aloofness is in some measure consequent to the profile pose, but it is attributable partly to the unbending character of the sitter, who in her husband's absence could rule their city state with iron hand.

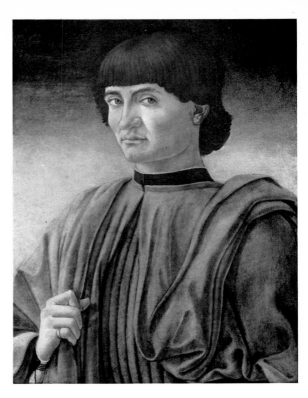

PORTRAIT OF A MAN
About 1455. By Castagno (Florentine)

WHETHER painted by Pollaiuolo or, as more critics believe, by his equally distinguished contemporary Castagno, this portrait is one of the greatest achievements of the Florentine 'scientific' painters. Without the aid of background view or other indication of surrounding space, the figure stands forth as solidly as if chiseled in stone. Strict discipline seems to hold in check a formidable vitality, ready to flash forth from the eyes turned on the spectator and implicit in the fingers clasped like a vice on the drapery. Something more than Florentine study of anatomy and perspective is responsible for this enhanced impression of life. Much is due to the artist's reformulation of nature's shapes, conspicuous in the strands of hair, that seem held forcibly in serried, rhythmic formation.

GIULIANO DE' MEDICI
About 1475. By Botticelli (Florentine)

R EPRESENTATION of palpable vitality was not enough to satisfy
Botticelli. He sought to express also the enigmatic merging of
opposing emotions, an experience which is usually keenest in adoles-
cence and is heightened in some of Botticelli's pictures to the point of
mysticism. At the time this portrait was painted, Giuliano de' Medici
seemed in every way the darling of fate. He was the idol of his family and
friends, glamorous tournament champion, and inspiration of the
brilliant poet Poliziano. Yet Botticelli has found in these proud and
haughty features a tinge of that sadness which seems so strangely
near in evanescent moments of greatest joy. Caught in the mysterious
spell of the painting, one feels in this shadow of sadness a prescience of
treacherous death so soon to overtake the handsome youth, victim of the
Pazzi conspirators.

63

PORTRAIT OF A YOUNG MAN
About 1475. By Antonello da Messina (Sicilian)

WHEN, in 1532, Marcantonio Michiel saw in Venice Antonello da Messina's portrait of Alvise Pasqualino—probably this very picture—he was impressed by the fact that it was 'painted in oil, in three-quarters view, highly finished, and of great power and vivacity, especially in the eyes.' Both the vivacious pose and the use of colors fused in oil may indicate an influence of Flemish artists, but the 'great power' of the portrait, its unapproachable reserve, bears witness to Antonello's contact with Piero della Francesca, the supreme master of detachment.

PORTRAIT OF A YOUNG MAN IN RED
About 1480. By Giovanni Bellini (Venetian)

E VEN before the Venetian visit, in 1475, of Antonello da Messina,
Bellini, like other artists in Venice, began to model with oil glazes.
But in this portrait he has depended for his shading chiefly on the old-
fashioned method of tempera hatching, so that the transitions from
light to dark are more abrupt than in the portrait by Antonello. In a
sense this method is well suited to the dramatic vein in Bellini's temperament. Though the eyes of this young man are fixed on the distance
instead of meeting ours as they do in Antonello's painting, there is no
barrier of reserve but, rather, a frank admittance of a nervous, excitable
temperament. To reinforce this mood, Bellini has substituted for
Antonello's plain background an Adriatic sky filled with threatening
clouds.

BIANCA MARIA SFORZA
Probably 1493. By Ambrogio de Predis (Milanese)

M ERITO ET TEMPORE (With Ability and Time). The jeweled ornament that bears this motto on Bianca Maria's headdress is a Sforza device, in the shape of a brush, symbolizing the promise of the usurping Sforza dukes of Milan to sweep Italy clean of evildoers. The masses of jewels loaded onto the young girl, painted at the time of her betrothal to Emperor Maximilian I, attest the might of her family rather than lend her beauty. In spite of her irregular features and unbecoming parure the portrait is beautiful. Carefully modeled with the delicate gradation of light and shade that de Predis learned from Leonardo, the homely Bianca reflects not a little the fascination of portraits by that great master.

PORTRAIT OF A LADY
About 1490. By Neroccio de' Landi (Sienese)

QVANTVM HOMINI FAS EST MIRA LICET ASSEQVAR ARTE: NIL AGO: MORTALIS EMVLOR ARTE DEOS (Permitted to reach what marvels in art a man may, I get nowhere, a mere mortal competing with the gods). With this distich at the bottom of his panel the artist extols the beauty of his young sitter. Her loveliness, and not family power, is the theme of the whole painting. The elaborate coiffure is designed to enhance the beauty of her features and the glowing pearl necklace encircles her throat like a tender caress. Though he was not, like Ambrogio de Predis, associated with Leonardo, Neroccio too reflects his influence, in the subtle modeling of face and hair, in the mobile lips, and in the river landscape, with its distant mountains bathed in opalescent light.

THE YOUNG ST. JOHN THE BAPTIST
About 1470. By Antonio Rossellino (Florentine)

ALTHOUGH the hair shirt on the left shoulder necessitates the label of 'St. John the Baptist' for this bust, it is clear that at the same time it is a portrait. Accepting it as such, we are struck by the precocity of the artist. Not until a generation later, with Giorgione and his circle, does painting succeed in capturing a transient mood as in this portrait. The slender, sensitively modeled features are still characteristic of the Quattrocento; not so the *contrapposto* of head and shoulders and the expression of quiet brooding.

PORTRAIT OF A YOUNG WOMAN AS A WISE VIRGIN
About 1510. By Sebastiano del Piombo (Venetian)

WHILE Rossellino's bust is a religious figure to which a portrait has been adapted, this painting is a portrait to which a religious symbol has been added. It is an early example of the kind of compliment which was to become popular, especially in the eighteenth century. Vittoria Colonna, poetess and friend of Michelangelo—for so tradition and a recently discovered inscription identify this young woman—was at the eve of her marriage when this portrait was painted, and what more fitting than to be shown as a Wise Virgin, with her lamp trimmed and burning! The dreamy, poetic mood is close to that of the little St. John, but the forms are now filled out and rounded, in keeping with the measured gestures and stately composure of the mature Renaissance.

PORTRAIT OF A YOUTH
About 1500. By Boltraffio (Milanese)

B OLTRAFFIO was Leonardo's principal pupil and follower. But even
for him this portrait is of such unusual excellence that one sur-
mises the master's personal supervision and finishing touch. In the soft,
wavy locks, the smooth, oval face, molded with subtle nuances of light
and shade, and in the clear, gentle eyes, we see an expression of two
significant ideals of the Italian Renaissance, formal beauty and intellectual control, which found their most harmonious fulfillment in
Leonardo's art. This calm Juno-like beauty may be taken as a goal
toward which the Italian experimenters of the fifteenth century were
striving in their reawakened awareness of the dignity of man.

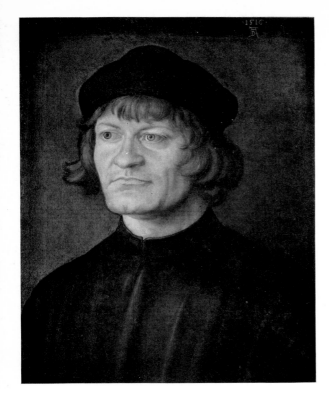

PORTRAIT OF A CLERGYMAN
Dated 1516. By Dürer (German)

To Germany, with her Reformation movement, the Renaissance
brought a new stimulation of conscience. Not awareness of the
dignity and importance of man, but awareness of his personal responsibility, was the principal driving force. Dürer's art, unlike Boltraffio's,
is intensely personal, though never used as propaganda. Dürer seems to
have found in this face, and in many another, an echo of his own earnest
questionings, his zealous search for truth (see Pl. 27). The piercing eyes,
firm mouth, furrowed jaw, swirling hair, and alert pose so bespeak a
daring thinker that the names of such prominent reformers as Johann
Dorsch and Ulrich Zwingli began long ago to be connected with this
portrait.

PORTRAIT OF A BOY (DETAIL FROM FIG. 17)
About 1540. By Bronzino (Florentine)

THE hands alone in this detail of an unknown lady and her son are an eloquent commentary on the court of Duke Cosimo II de' Medici. The little boy's hand touches that of his mother, but the touch is merely a convention; there is no response in their long, artificially smooth fingers. It is enough for our purpose to show only one of the faces in the double portrait, for both were cast in Bronzino's mold of comely but melancholy masks. One would think the whole entourage of the duke, whom Bronzino painted in their stiff, rich brocades, were burdened with Cosimo's secrets of deceit and treachery and dared not betray their feelings, even—and especially—to their nearest of kin.

PARVVLE PATRISSA, PATRIÆ, VIRTVTIS ET HÆRES
ESTO, NIHIL MAIVS MAXIMVS ORBIS HABET.
GNATVM VIX POSSVNT COELVM ET NATVRA DEDISSE,
HVIVS QVEM PATRIS, VICTVS HONORET HONOS.
Æ.QVATO TANTVM, TANTI TV FACTA PARENTIS,
VOTA HOMINVM, VIX QVO PROGREDIANTVR, HABENT.
VINCITO, VICISTI, QVOT REGES PRISCVS ADORAT
ORBIS, NEC TE QVI VINCERE POSSIT, ERIT.

EDWARD VI AS A CHILD
1538. By Holbein the Younger (German)

IN smooth, enamel-like finish Bronzino vies with his great German contemporary Holbein, and both are known best as portrait painters. But how different their conception of portraiture! With Holbein there is no question of a typical mold. Each sitter offered a new challenge. Each was a unique person, the essentials of whose appearance the painter had to grasp and record. So absorbing was the pursuit that the artist's emotional reactions to the sitter—if he had any—were completely excluded. From the painting of little Prince Edward one learns nothing of Holbein's attitude toward the royal family, but one learns a great deal about the appearance of the baby. The portrait was painted for presentation to Henry VIII on New Year's Day, 1539. The royal father repaid the artist with a golden goblet.

73

DOGE ANDREA GRITTI
About 1538. By Titian (Venetian)

As painter to the doges of Venice, Titian repeatedly portrayed Andrea Gritti. In this last portrait of the series, along with the features and personality of the sitter, the artist took into account Gritti's brilliant career, his military and diplomatic triumphs and the cultural splendor of his long rule. The result is the most imposing portrait ever painted by Titian. It probably belongs to the very end of the doge's eighty-three years, but the dignity and majesty of old age rather than its weakness speak from the stern features and proud bearing. With the swirl of drapery across the breast and the broad movement of the hand, Titian pays tribute to Michelangelo, supreme master in sculpture, as he himself was supreme in painting.

TITIAN'S SCHOOLMASTER'
'About 1575. By Moroni (Brescian)

BECAUSE of an early attribution this portrait is still called 'Titian's Schoolmaster.' But we do not know whether the sitter is a school-master, and we do know that the artist is not Titian. The painting is particularly unlike such a formal, state portrait as Titian's Andrea Gritti. In the 'Schoolmaster' there is no suggestion of pomp and cir-cumstance. So unobstrusive is the costume that we notice only the snowy white collar, while plain fact rather than imposing effect is conveyed by the head and hands. Both pose and motive are simple and casual: a scholar looks up for a moment from his reading. Still immersed in his thought, he is scarcely conscious of the spectator and does not prepare his expression for public view, but remains relaxed as if he were alone. So, as our eyes meet his, we seem to look into the unguarded precincts of a fellow-soul and we experience a heightened awareness of our humanity.

RANUCCIO FARNESE
1542. By Titian (Venetian)

M OST of Titian's paintings, and especially his portraits, evoke the elegant court life of his day. He was painter to princes of church and state even from the beginning of his career. Noble bearing was as normal to his conception of a figure as were the rich colors with which he painted it. What we see in this charming portrait is not so much an individual boy as a typical Italian prince of the mid-sixteenth century. And we are not surprised to learn that the boy was already prior of the Knights of Malta when painted here at the age of eleven, and that he was bishop at thirteen and archbishop at fourteen.

PORTRAIT OF A LADY WITH AN OSTRICH-FEATHER FAN
About 1660. By Rembrandt (Dutch)

ALONG with the great Jan Six in Amsterdam, this painting stands at the pinnacle of Rembrandt's achievement in portraiture. Even among his scores of masterly portraits these two are exceptional for their direct presentation. They show little of Titian's emphasis on class and little indication of time and place. Our now anonymous lady, like Jan Six, must have been well known to Rembrandt, and yet not so intimately as to lead him into her subconscious problems. This explains the amazing unity of the portrait. The same vivid personality is expressed in every detail, in the hands—these most wonderfully painted hands in all art—as unmistakably as in the face.

SELF-PORTRAIT
About 1488. By Lorenzo di Credi (Florentine)

'WHEN the brief days of spring toward summer sink. . . .' With this note of regret, in one of his best poems, Lorenzo de' Medici voiced the pensive mood of the humanistic circle in fifteenth-century Florence. It is the mood that Lorenzo di Credi, at about the age of thirty, saw in his mirror. His youthful grace and beauty (unconsciously idealized, no doubt), silhouetted against the dewy light of the distant landscape, seemed but a reminder of the brevity of the springtime of life—and his spirit filled with a vague sadness.

SELF-PORTRAIT
Dated 1659. By Rembrandt (Dutch)

SEVENTEENTH-CENTURY Holland was far too busy to indulge in vague dreams of vanishing youth. Rembrandt left nearly a hundred self-portraits, and each is a fresh, probing study of his character and physical appearance. Beside their revelation the other documents of his life pale in significance. When we stand before this great portrait, painted in his fifty-third year, the stories of business failure and unconventional living that have gathered round his memory seem but petty, ungrateful gossip. In the quiet, controlled face, with its penetrating, unflinching eyes, we see acceptance of what life has brought and compassion born of tragic sorrow.

A PRINCESS OF THE HOUSE OF ARAGON
About 1475. By Francesco da Laurana (Italian)

I N that springtime of the Italian Renaissance, when youth and beauty reigned, no artist achieved a purer distillation of feminine loveliness than did Laurana in his marble busts of women. They are much alike, with only the slightest individual characterization, so their anonymity does not matter. Moreover, such perfect symmetry, such crystal-clear contour and flow of surface were not to be found in any living model. Even the decoration of the base of this bust, with its reliefs of centaurs and Herculean *putti*, takes us away from reality and the accidents of time and place.

A YOUNG GIRL WITH A FLUTE
About 1660. By Vermeer (Dutch)

WOMEN were as frequently represented by Vermeer as by Laurana and the two artists were equally indifferent to the personality of their sitters. But at what unlike results they arrived! Here is such recognition of the accidents of time and place as could rank Vermeer in the vanguard of the Impressionists. Leaning far to one side of the composition, undisciplined by Laurana's carefully planned symmetry, this girl seems to be shown just as the artist found her, sitting at a window, with the dancing sunlight and shadows distorting her features and transforming the projections on dress and chair into a mass of jewels that vie with the pearls at her ears. For light, not the *beau ideal*, was Vermeer's theme, and it is light that reigns supreme in this picture.

QUINTILIA FISCHIERI
About 1580. By Barocci (Marchegian)

SENSITIVE, like other Mannerists, to a variety of influences, Barocci sometimes reminds us vaguely of Raphael and of Correggio. But he represents a new style, carried further by his younger contemporary El Greco; and his pictures were noted with profit by Rubens and Van Dyck, and by many lesser artists. The exaggerated movement which often dominates his religious compositions gives place in his rare portraits to a quiet reserve that borders on repression. Although we read here, on the folded paper, that Quintilia Fischieri, an Urbinate like Barocci himself, was the artist's patron, she seems very childlike, with her dainty features and delicate, transparent skin. The fresh, pastel effect of Barocci's luminous, changeable colors was his own inimitable invention.

PAOLA ADORNO, MARCHESA BRIGNOLE SALE, AND HER SON
About 1625. By Van Dyck (Flemish)

H IS idol Titian was not the only source of inspiration for that burst
of exuberance in which Van Dyck worked during his Genoese
period. Some of his portraits of children suggest the immediate example
of Barocci, whose delicate painting of flesh and mannered elongation of
figure must have been particularly congenial to Van Dyck. But that Van
Dyck reached his zenith in the Paola Adorno and other portraits of that
brilliant Genoese galaxy must be attributed partly to the artist's appreciation and approval of his sitters. He painted the nobility all his life,
but their nobility seemed to him more genuine in Italy than elsewhere.
These high-born ladies find a perfect setting in the sunny gardens and
marble palaces of the Italian Riviera. And the smile that lurks on their
lips, is it not a memento of Van Dyck's delight in their vivacity and
warmth?

ST. BURCHARD OF WÜRZBURG
About 1515. By Riemenschneider (German)

WHILE his great German contemporaries Dürer and Peter Vischer the Younger were as enthusiastic champions of the Renaissance as we may find outside of Italy, Riemenschneider was loath to break away from mediaeval tradition. Frequently his figures, cut in wood or stone, stand in a swaying Gothic pose, their robes agitated by a multiplicity of angular folds that sometimes fly out gustily. But this portrait of a bishop, which belongs to the sculptor's mature period, shows the Renaissance gaining ground. The drapery has become simpler, and there is a relaxing of the mediaeval tenseness, especially in the noble, serious face.

LOUIS XIV

About 1665. By Bernini (Roman)

THE Baroque style, of which Bernini was one of the great exponents, might seem at first thought a throwback to the late Gothic style. But the differences between the two are fundamental. The multiple folds and the undulating locks, sometimes almost as extravagant in Riemenschneider as in Bernini, are in the former a decorative setting, in the latter, an expression of the main theme. In Riemenschneider they are like the richly jeweled shrine of a sacred relic; in Bernini, like the burgeoning of a luxuriant plant. The ascetic bishop has no spiritual relation to his ornamented costume. Louis XIV's curled wig, embroidered jabot, and billowing drapery are worldly heralds of his worldly grandeur. Like the self-assured tilt of his chin, the proud glance of his eye, and the half-scornful curl of his lip, they bespeak his sense of kingly might and right. Surely no other style could have suited this proud monarch so well as the Baroque.

JOSEPH BONNIER DE LA MOSSON
Dated 1745. By Nattier (French)

I N the sparkling society of mid-eighteenth-century France, while the
great ladies were posing in the guise of Hebe or Diana, the fashion-
able men chose to appear as fastidious dilettanti. The spirit of the
'Enlightenment' was in the air. Diderot and his fellow-Encyclopedists
were girding themselves for their vast undertaking when this portrait
was painted, and Buffon was preparing his famous *Histoire Naturelle*.
The book which Bonnier de la Mosson leans on bears this title, and
samples of his extensive collection of scientific instruments and medical
specimens are displayed in the background. Like his sumptuous dress,
carved furniture, and assured manner, his collection could testify to his
distinguished position in the society of his time. Rarely has the spirit of
this society been more successfully expressed.

MONSIEUR DE LA LIVE DE JULLY
Probably 1759. By Greuze (French)

A T court La Live de Jully was Introducer of Ambassadors. In private
life he was an enthusiastic dilettante, in the practice of art as well
as in connoisseurship. Here, in his elegant lounging robe, he is the
amateur musician. The portfolio and statuette in the background remind us of his other accomplishments. He was an amateur engraver and
passionate collector of French art, largely ordered from living artists.
Conspicuous in the room where he sits at his harp are examples of the
furniture *à la grec* which he commissioned a decade before the return of
that Louis XIV style to popularity. And this portrait itself, always
recognized as the artist's masterpiece, is La Live de Jully's reward for
his liberal patronage of Greuze.

MARCHESA ELENA GRIMALDI,
WIFE OF MARCHESE NICOLA CATTANEO
Probably 1623. By Van Dyck (Flemish)

THE secret of Van Dyck's brilliant success as a portraitist is his interpretation of aristocracy. Luxuriant landscape, a glorious sky, marble columns, splendid costuming form the setting for Elena Grimaldi, and we feel that nothing less magnificent would be suitable for her. There is no haughtiness or disdain in her bearing—she would smile sweetly on her devoted servant if she should turn. Her natural superiority is completely disarming and we accept it gladly, even enthusiastically. Small wonder that Van Dyck was a favorite portrait painter wherever he went!

L'ANDALOUSE
About 1898. By Whistler (American)

WHISTLER'S preference for the full-length, elongated figure in portraiture recalls Van Dyck. But his intention was very different, as his title for this picture announces. This is a portrait of Mrs. Whibley, the artist's sister-in-law; but he calls her L'Andalouse, wishing to conceal her identity and her station in life. She merely served as model for a carefully wrought pattern, her sweeping figure perfectly framed within the narrow boundaries of the canvas. The pearly gray wall balancing the darker area of the floor, the famous butterfly signature placed with delicate precision at the right, and even the unusual pose of the figure—all these features of the beautifully patterned arrangement owe something to the example of Japanese prints, but are none the less products of Whistler's fastidious taste.

GEORGIANA, DUCHESS OF DEVONSHIRE
1783. By Gainsborough (British)

THE merit of the eighteenth-century English portraitists lies chiefly in their decorative felicity. Though something of the Van Dyck tradition remained, artists like Gainsborough adapted it to a new clientele. Their patrons were the nobility and the gentry, living comfortably and leisurely in vast houses set in landscaped parks. Portraits were wanted as evidence of complacent living and as decoration for spacious, sunny drawing rooms. Witty and clever the Duchess of Devonshire may have been, but the artist sought in her only what could contribute to the grace and luxury of the composition.

MARQUESA DE PONTEJOS
1785/90. By Goya (Spanish)

O BVIOUSLY, Goya had in mind both his English and his French
contemporaries when he painted this portrait. And no doubt he
felt a slight scorn for the complacency of the one and the artificiality of
the other. One can almost fancy this marquesa a Gainsborough lady
who has snapped from her languor into sudden attention, or a Fragonard
coquette who for once has ceased her tinkling laughter. Most of all, one
marvels that the marquesa could have accepted in her portrait such
mockery of her high-born caste. But Goya created his own fashion and,
besides, the marquesa may have been intelligent enough to value superb
painting above flattery.

THE SKATER

1782. By Stuart (American)

THIS brilliant painting, little known until recently, brings a sharp answer to those critics who have doubted Stuart's adequacy as a painter of full-length figures. It is true that most of his hundreds of patrons—chiefly Americans—were satisfied with a bust, or with a half-length at most. For what they had in mind was merely a likeness. The unusual commission to paint this full-length came early in Stuart's career, when he was in London and under the influence of British decorative portraitists like Gainsborough and Romney. In an exhibition a century later The Skater was even mistaken for the work of one of these two British artists or of Raeburn. It is a portrait of the Scottish gentleman William Grant of Congalton skating on the lake in St. James Park, London.

CAPTAIN PATRICK MILLER
About 1795. By Raeburn (British)

THE influence upon Stuart of his British contemporaries was not without reciprocation. Two years after Stuart had painted and exhibited The Skater, Raeburn painted a portrait of a skater, now in the National Gallery of Scotland. Even some of Raeburn's later work, this equestrian portrait, for example, is not far from Stuart's style. There is a similar freshness and spontaneity in the paintings of the two artists, and a similar decorative use of broad brush strokes for accent. The subject of this portrait, a captain in the Dumfriesshire Yeomanry, was the son of Patrick Miller, projector of steam navigation, and one-time friend and landlord of Robert Burns at the Miller estate of Dalswinton, Dumfries-shire, Scotland.

THE CHRIST CHILD

About 1460. By Desiderio da Settignano (Florentine)

EVEN after five hundred years we sense in the sculptor of this portrait bust a contemporary spirit. That we do so is partly owing to the timeless appeal of childhood, but more to a common cultural heritage, rooted in Classical antiquity. The very form of this portraiture, the sculptured bust, is an echo from ancient Rome. Desiderio developed it in the direction of extreme subtlety of expression. The sensitive modeling of this face gives in every feature such an impression of mobility, of blossoming smile, as one expects to find nowhere outside a painting or drawing by Leonardo. Fascinated by the human aspect, one might never guess the religious purpose of the bust were it not evident that a halo was once attached to the crown of the head.

ALEXANDRE BRONGNIARD
Dated 1777. By Houdon (French)

THREE centuries pass, and we are again in a period of Classical revival, before we find another sculptor who could vie with Desiderio and his Florentine contemporaries in the portraiture of children. There is, to be sure, a difference of approach. Desiderio looked at his living model over the shoulder, so to speak, of his Classical predecessors. Houdon studied his model directly, Classical example serving him merely as discipline. There is evidence of that discipline in the reserve and simplicity of this bust and in such conventions as the deep carving of hair and eyes. But Houdon's sculptural emphasis upon anatomical structure in contrast to Desiderio's pictorial emphasis upon surface modulation marks Houdon as an artist of the scientific age and reminds us that his early anatomical study, the famous *Ecorché*, still serves as a model for art students.

MADAME BERGERET
Dated 1746. By Boucher (French)

THE charm of the vast decorations Boucher was to carry out for Madame de Pompadour is anticipated in this early portrait. Its luxuriant abundance—of silken drapery, of fleecy clouds, of flowers at their full bloom—was to become characteristic of Boucher's settings, not only for portraits of women but for mythologies too (see Pl. 49). His pupil Fragonard, by increasing the proportionate size of the setting, was to emphasize the daintiness and fragility of the figure, but at the loss of Boucher's almost Classical restraint (see Pls. 120 and 149). Madame Bergeret and her husband were among the earliest patrons of Boucher and Fragonard, and her brother was the famous Abbé de Saint-Non who accompanied Fragonard and Hubert Robert on their momentous trip to Italy in the 1760's.

NAPOLEON IN HIS STUDY
Dated 1812. By Jacques-Louis David (French)

P LACING the fragile Madame Bergeret beside the solid Napoleon may seem like grouping a Tanagra figurine with the statue of a Roman emperor. Yet David was long and strongly influenced by Boucher. From this master he learned to enliven his flesh tones with small flecks of varying colors. And Boucher's Classical reserve, clear modeling, and mythological bent must have encouraged David in his espousal of the Neoclassical cause in French Revolutionary art. But Boucher's rose garlands and billowing drapery find no echo in the severely designed setting of this official portrait, a setting insistent in every detail upon the emperor's omnipotence. Noticing the clock and the far-spent candle in the picture, Napoleon thus expressed his approval: 'You have understood me, David, by night I work for the welfare of my subjects, and by day for their glory.'

97

MADAME DAVID
Dated 1813. By Jacques-Louis David (French)

'THOUGH her features were not regular, liveliness of complexion and expression gave her countenance a charming animation,' a grandson wrote of David's wife. And we may rest assured that David has shown her just as she was. For, although he preached Classicism and painted historical pictures in a cold, Classical style, his best portraits are masterly records of direct observation, spontaneous in effect, as if painted in a single sitting.

MADAME MOITESSIER (DETAIL)
Dated 1851. By Ingres (French)

'NEVER did beauty more regal, more splendid, more superb, and of a type more Junonian yield its proud lineaments to the trembling crayons of an artist,' wrote Théophile Gautier after watching Madame Moitessier pose for her portrait. Gautier's resounding tribute is echoed in Ingres' painting. Trained under David, Ingres never ceased striving to attain the Classical ideal. He sought it not only in ancient art and the paintings of Raphael but, above all, in nature. He began making sketches of Madame Moitessier four years before he finally finished this portrait —changing her pose, altering her coiffure, redrawing her features. Not spontaneous effect, but absolute composure, clean contour, precise modeling, and unity of composition were his goal.

THE MOTHER AND SISTER OF THE ARTIST
1869/70. By Morisot (French)

I T was principally Manet who initiated Berthe Morisot into the mysteries of Impressionism. In this picture he gave her a demonstration of his personal technique by retouching the dress and head of Madame Morisot. But Manet's early preference for sombre colors was not shared by his young friend, nor did she later follow extreme Impressionists like Monet in sacrificing form and local color to the dazzling brilliance of light. Her greatest charm is indeed her painting of light, but her light is disciplined by early training under Corot and retains something of his pearly quality. For the sake of luminous effects on folds and ruffles of white muslin she would pose a white-clad model in a sunny landscape or on the quay or, as here, in the center of an evenly lighted room, where shadows would find slight accent.

THE DUKE AND DUCHESS OF MORBILLI
About 1865. By Degas (French)

DEGAS was a keen observer, but he could not accept the Impressionists' faith in the finality of visual impressions. His intellectual approach made him analyse what he saw. Selecting essentials, he recreated instead of copying. And over this process his uncompromising sense of fitness presided, a sense developed in an atelier still dominated by the discipline of Ingres' drawing, but modified by the study of Venetian color in the museums and by the impact of a new concept of design in the Japanese prints reaching Paris. Except for the rich color and freedom of technique, the portrait of the artist's sister in this painting, or that of her husband, might have been done by Ingres; but such surprises as the arrangement of the sitters at different levels have a new, Japanese flavor. Never satisfied, Degas scraped out the hands and scarf of the duchess, and the picture remained unfinished in his studio.

PORTRAIT OF AN ELDERLY LADY
Dated 1633. By Frans Hals (Dutch)

WHEN this unknown lady sat for her portrait, Holland was exultant with victory. Prosperity and well-being were the order of the day, and Hals as an artist, whatever his private troubles, was in tune with the prevailing mood. Portraiture filled his whole career, partly because of the demand, but chiefly, no doubt, because he found his cheerful, self-satisfied sitters congenial to his style of painting. His brilliant mastery of technique achieves a spontaneity that seems the very essence of life. This elderly lady, we are convinced, must have been exactly as she appears here. Just so she must have kept her eyes on the artist through a brief sitting. Brief, indeed, for her hand grips the chair as if she were about to rise and start again her vigorous round of activity.

LA MOUSMÉ
1888. By Van Gogh (Dutch)

AFTER two hundred and fifty years came along another Dutch artist to paint with bold, broad strokes, which might seem the ultimate development of the virtuosity of Hals. But actually Van Gogh learned little from Hals and was no heir to his technical facility. With none of the gay bravura of Hals, Van Gogh labored with a religious, even fanatical, but anxious, zeal, his brush never ceasing to be an unfamiliar tool in his hand. For instantaneous effect the Elderly Lady by Hals is impressionistic enough for the artists of Van Gogh's day, while the perennial tragedy of life, read into the face of this Japanese girl through the creative agony of the artist, gives La Mousmé a monumentality that reigns over the strident color and awkward pose.

PUTTO POISED ON A GLOBE
About 1485. By Verrocchio (Florentine)

THIS terracotta figure might classify as mythology or as genre. If we imagine a bow in his right hand, from which he has just let fly an arrow, then this is the love god Cupid. But his childish abandon, his soft, chubby body, and his curly locks tossed by the wind describe a typical baby at play. The original purpose of the figure, as well as the intended subject, is unknown. Possibly it is a study for the fountain figure which Verrocchio was commissioned, shortly before his death, to make for Matthias Corvinus of Hungary.

CHILD ON A DOLPHIN
About 1515. By Peter Vischer the Younger (German)

THE Italian use of *putti* as decorative motives may have set the
example for the profusion of baby figures that clamber and play over
the great bronze monuments cast by the Vischer family. But it is of the
world of elves and gnomes that these German figures remind us, rather
than of Classical mythology. This roguish boy is prying at the jaws of a
dolphin, which curls up its tail to form a nice saddle. The puffy legs and
arms, and the clumps of stiff hair are not quite typical of a child; to make
it more exotic, Vischer has hung a pear-shaped pendant from one ear
and a large ring from the other.

SHEPHERDS (DETAIL FROM THE NATIVITY, FIG. 3)
About 1445. By Petrus Christus (Flemish)

ALTHOUGH genre subjects, views of everyday life, did not thrive independently in art before the seventeenth century, they were frequent as a kind of byplay in religious scenes and elsewhere. In this detail from the Nativity there is no addition to the usual *dramatis personae*, only a revision of some of the rôles. Instead of listening to the angelic announcement or kneeling in adoration, these shepherds are curious and amused, make comments, and look in through the windows like children peering onto a stage from behind the scenes. Ordinary folk, they must wear warm caps and heavy cloaks against the winter's cold, but the Virgin kneels with uncovered head and the Christ Child, though nude on the bare ground, is radiant.

SPECTATORS (DETAIL FROM THE ADORATION OF THE MAGI, PL. 9)
About 1445. By Fra Angelico and Fra Filippo Lippi (Florentine)

To emphasize the vulgar status of the group of onlookers who crowd forward and jostle one another here, particularly crude, homely models seem to have been chosen. One scarcely thinks of models in connection with the highly idealized figures in the religious scene below. But for the motley rabble the artist must have bethought himself of the beggars he commonly saw on the streets of Florence. To similar observation we owe the group of nude boys so gratuitously introduced on the level above—bathers, perhaps, who have come running to get a glimpse of the spectacle. Their well-drawn bodies bear witness to the interest in anatomical and life studies in fifteenth-century Florence.

THE CARD PLAYERS
About 1520. By Lucas van Leyden (Dutch)

I N genre painting Lucas van Leyden was a century ahead of his time. Among his contemporaries, Dürer sometimes approached genre, but commonly with a suggestion of allegory. Van Leyden's Card Players seems to have no ulterior meaning. Except for the costumes, typical of the artist's day, this might be any group of card players at any time. Their expressions are rigidly typical, and it would never occur to us to want to identify the sitters. The air of casualness is heightened by the accessories: the refreshments laid out on table and ledge (see Pl. 123), the coins tossed in careless heaps, and the gaily colored garments.

THE DANCING COUPLE
Dated 1663. By Steen (Dutch)

I T is a happy coincidence that Steen's birthplace is the same as that of
Lucas van Leyden. For of all the great seventeenth-century Dutch
masters of genre, Steen is the most direct heir of Lucas' style in this
category. But Steen's scenes are more complicated than those of the
older master. He is rarely satisfied with one episode. All sorts of byplay
are added, partly as complement and partly as comment, to the central
theme. Steen's perennial delight in scenes of rollicking fun may stem
from his student days at the University of Leyden. But his excellent
technique, which wins him comparison at times with Vermeer, bespeaks
a more sober and industrious youth than his subjects might suggest.

A FRENCH INTERIOR
About 1645. By Louis Le Nain (French)

IN contrast to the unbiased approach of such an artist as Lucas van Leyden (see Pl. 107), there may seem to be an emphasis upon poverty and piety by Louis Le Nain. Yet he does not anticipate the sentimentality of Greuze, who was in some respects his thematic descendant. This interior, with all the detail of ragged garments, wrinkled faces, unkempt hair, and the clutter of an overcrowded room, is transformed into a scene of dignity and beauty by the solemn air of quiet suspense and by the strong contrasts of light and shade, of which Caravaggio, in Italy, had shown all Europe the secret.

THE OLD MUSICIAN
Dated 1862. By Manet (French)

ONLY superficially does this painting come into the category of genre. Instead of a *typical* scene, such as Le Nain gives us, we seem to have here a series of portraits. One can hardly speak of these figures as forming a group; each is studied for its individual appearance, and there is only sparing indication of the setting. Le Nain undertook to tell something about the life of a social class. When Manet, two hundred years later, painted the same class of people, he did not comment on their status. He was concerned exclusively with his visual impressions.

A WOMAN WEIGHING GOLD
About 1657. By Vermeer (Dutch)

It was simple; it came of itself alone,
As the darkness falls when the day is done.

VICTOR Hugo's acceptance of nature's mysteries rises to mind when we look at a painting by Vermeer. In this picture he commemorates the daily miracle of sunlight. The golden flood filters through the half-curtained window of the gold-weigher's room to bathe the exposed surfaces, each according to its texture and its angle. So convincing is this lighting, so inevitable the placing of the figure within the space of the room, so just the balance between the woman's attention and her action, that the picture defies analysis and classification. Is this portraiture, genre, still life, or even allegory, the weighing of gold echoing the weighing of souls in the scene of the Last Judgment on the wall?

A DUTCH COURTYARD
About 1660. By de Hooch (Dutch)

S UBJECT is more important with de Hooch than with Vermeer. He too is an excellent painter of light, but of light not so much for its own sake as for its interpretative and expressive utility. In this courtyard scene, as in most other paintings of his best period, de Hooch's theme is the pleasantness of home, where family and friends, engaged in quiet sociability or in domestic activities, escape from the alien distraction of the outer world. This picture reflects the charm of those magic days, rare in Holland even in summer, when the sun breaks through the clouds and mist. The vertical shadows show that the sun has reached the zenith and is starting on its decline to the western horizon, with the tower of Delft's New Church athwart its path.

A GIRL WITH A BROOM
Dated 1651. By Rembrandt (Dutch)

MANY of Rembrandt's compositions, especially his biblical ones, wear the outward semblance of genre. Yet one hesitates to include in that category even this painting of a young servant. Appropriate accessories of everyday life are here—broom, bucket, informal dress, and the rough window ledge over which the girl leans out into the sunlight. Yet even the menial equipment does not dispose us to speculate on her particular station in life. For we see in her not a human type, the serving girl, but a human being, subject to suffering and joy, so sympathetic and understanding is Rembrandt's interpretation.

THE NEEDLEWOMAN
About 1640. By Velázquez (Spanish)

G ENRE is as doubtful a category in the case of Velázquez as of
Rembrandt, though on very different grounds. Rembrandt is too
personal for genre, Velázquez too impersonal. Neither what people
think nor what they do seems to have any interest for Velázquez. This
young woman happens to be sewing, but we do not think of the picture
as a typical representation of that activity. It enthralls us by the magic
of its light, the subtle modeling of its forms, the distillation, as it were,
of the qualities of textiles, hair, and flesh.

A GIRL AND HER DUENNA
About 1665/75. By Murillo (Spanish)

NEITHER very profound nor very original, Murillo is now generally more acceptable in his portrait and genre subjects than in his formerly prized religious compositions. Even in genre he is often a bit sentimental or artificial, insisting on prettiness, and sweetness of pose and expression. But occasionally, as in this painting, he composes with simplicity and sincerity, and only the over-sophisticated could object to the story-telling implications of the scene. The young girl leaning on the sill is charmingly portrayed, with great beauty of technique and a fine sense of color harmony. The picture has sometimes been called Las Gallegas, from the popular fabrication that Murillo's models were two notorious courtesans, sisters who came to Seville from Galicia.

THE HOUSE OF CARDS
Probably 1735. By Chardin (French)

WITH Chardin there is never even a suggestion of sentimentality. This is the more remarkable in that his subjects were usually children and people in lowly walks of life. But while his contemporary Jean-Jacques Rousseau sentimentalized on the innocence and virtue of these people, Chardin was busy recording the varying blue of a ribbon as the light played over it, or the subtle profile of a figure, now merging into the background, now silhouetted more sharply. The shadow of a knob on the table drawer, the glint of a button on the sleeve, the pastel-like beauty of the colors, and the agreeably crumbly texture of the paint were more important to Chardin's purpose than was the identity or character of his model.

THE KITCHEN MAID
Dated 1738. By Chardin (French)

I T was Chardin's great merit that he expressed the essence of visual
experience. An actual woman seated in a chair could not compete
with this painting in making us aware of a space as occupied by a body,
of a hand in its capability to grasp, of a lap as a means of support. We
delight in the weight of the dress, in the solidity of the chair, and in the
porous texture of the turnips in the bowl. It is amazing how aware
Chardin makes us of each object, its material, its form, its color, and its
exact relationship to everything else in the picture. And it is amazing
what pleasure we take in that awareness.

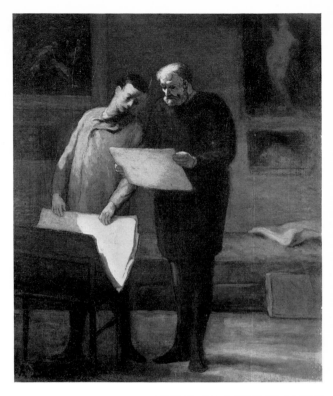

ADVICE TO A YOUNG ARTIST
About 1860. By Daumier (French)

A s Chardin brings us the essence of visual experience, Daumier presents the essence of human behavior. In subjects that easily become sentimental and trivial each had the genius to discover elements of universal significance. Through most of his career Daumier turned out for journals a daily quota of caricatures that rise to the realm of fine art. The figures and episodes in his drawings, lithographs, and paintings are not merely symbols of human foibles and passions. They are individuals and events that mirror mankind so sympathetically that, while we may smile at some absurdity or shake our heads over some exposure of fraud, we are never left without a touch of fellow-feeling. Daumier has contrasted intellectual concentration in this towering critic with intellectual pliability in the young artist bending toward him. How expressive the simple poses, and how monumental the composition!

A GAME OF PIGNATTA
About 1760. By Pietro Longhi (Venetian)

In Venice, the cultural center of Italy in the eighteenth century, the chief demands in secular art were for portraiture and large wall decorations. Longhi was an exception in devoting his attention to genre. He adapted his exquisitely painted scenes of elegant society to the smaller, more intimate rooms in the palaces. The people in his pictures never let themselves go, as they do in Dutch genre. In this naïve game a blindfolded man politely strikes at an overturned kitchen kettle while the onlookers are restrained in their enthusiasm, some perhaps only pretending to be absorbed in the play. The figures move like actors on a stage, and their silks and laces glisten as if under artificial light.

BLINDMAN'S BUFF (DETAIL)
About 1765. By Fragonard (French)

L ONGHI reminds us of the studied unreality of the theater. Fragonard takes us into a world of dizzy, coquettish abandon. In far-reaching parks, under towering trees, the tiny figures flit breathlessly, tingle at each other's touch as they pass, but never stop to look attentively, one into the face of another. This blindfolded girl and her companions take only a small part of the great canvas (see the pendant, Pl. 149), and with a few brilliant strokes, in contrast to Longhi's careful finish, Fragonard has caught the spirit of vibrant frivolity.

STILL LIFE (DETAIL FROM THE ANNUNCIATION, FIG. 6)
About 1425. By Jan van Eyck (Flemish)

ALTHOUGH well known from ancient times, still life as an independent category could scarcely satisfy the grave ideals of the Middle Ages, nor yet the heroic aspirations of the Renaissance. It could find an incidental place, however, in accepted subjects. The lilies beside the Virgin in van Eyck's Annunciation are intended, to be sure, to symbolize her purity, and the stool suggests her humility. But, for all that, van Eyck has recorded with a still-life painter's delight the silky smoothness of the petals, the soft glow of the cut velvet, and the sturdiness of the richly grained oak. The play of light over the surfaces and the shadows cast on the intarsia pavement give an almost *trompe-l'oeil* effect to the stool and its cushion.

THE CHALICE OF ST. JOHN THE EVANGELIST
(BACK OF THE ST. VERONICA PANEL, PL. 132)
About 1470. By Memling (Flemish)

ONE of the very few independent still lifes preserved from the
fifteenth century is this picture of a chalice set in a niche. It is
painted on the back of a small diptych panel, where the artist could
indulge his fancy, as in the predella of an altarpiece. On the front of the
panel is St. Veronica (see Pl. 132); and the pendant must have been St.
John the Evangelist, whose emblem, the chalice from which poison
issued in the form of a serpent, was visible when the diptych was closed.
Contemplating the closed diptych, the owner must frequently have
turned from thoughts of symbolic significance to enjoyment of the
picture as pure still life, the beautifully painted chalice glowing like
polished metal where the light seems to strike it in its simulated niche.

STILL LIFE (DETAIL FROM THE CARD PLAYERS, PL. 107)
About 1520. By Lucas van Leyden (Dutch)

ALTHOUGH the Germanized figures of Lucas van Leyden almost belie his nationality, his still-life arrangements and genre subjects (see Pl. 107) are prophetically Dutch and mark him as an innovator. If he had devoted a whole panel or canvas to this table set out so attractively with vases, flowers, cheese box, and pear, it could take its place among the fine Dutch still lifes painted in the seventeenth century. It would even be at home with the Chardins, of the eighteenth century, and the Cézannes, of the nineteenth (see Pls. 129, 130).

STILL LIFE
About 1665. By Kalf (Dutch)

IN seventeenth-century Holland a prosperous middle class that
delighted in sensuously beautiful objects provided the most congenial atmosphere for still-life painting that artists have ever known.
The subject of Kalf's late pictures, food and wine on a table, was
common in the still lifes of the time. But no others are so consistently
elegant and rich as his. These wine glasses, the phoenix-topped hanaper,
blue-figured Japanese bowl, and Turkey carpet are collectors' items.
The wonder is that the artist could be content to half lose the costly
objects in shadow. It is, however, just this—his poetic control of light,
perhaps inspired by Rembrandt—that makes Kalf great.

STILL LIFE
About 1600. By Caravaggio (Roman)

STILL life as an independent pictorial genre, which was to find great favor in Northern art, was early practised in Italy by the great figure painter Caravaggio. He not only made still life a prominent accessory in his figure pictures but also painted it by itself and with the same care for form and texture that he devoted to the human body. 'Caravaggio said,' reported an incredulous contemporary, 'that it was just as difficult for him to produce a good picture of flowers as one of figures.' His still lifes are more, too, than displays of objects: his sombre view of existence is expressed in the deep shadows and in the signs of inescapable decay in the bursting fruits.

STILL LIFE

Dated 1627. By Juan van der Hamen y Leon (Spanish)

NOT much later than Caravaggio's still life is this one by the young Hamen y Leon, who set the style for still-life painting in Spain. Some of the objects he repeatedly paints may recall his Northern parentage. The wooden cheese boxes, for instance, are like those shown by Lucas van Leyden (Pls. 107, 123), and some of the glass would no doubt have been acceptable to the later Dutch master Kalf (Pl. 124). The abundance and variety of objects in the picture may be a further indication of Northern taste. But there is an air of formality and seriousness in the painting that reveals Juan's Spanish environment. In Flanders and Holland these stone blocks would have seemed bare and hard—even the Realist Caravaggio, in Italy, would have covered them with linen. And the display of the objects in formal rows has a kind of austere solemnity that was to become more marked in the rare still lifes of Spain's great figure painters.

STILL LIFE
(DETAIL FROM 'DIANE DE POITIERS,' FRONTISPIECE)
About 1570. By François Clouet (French)

A s a good story-teller sometimes interrupts the flow of his story to dwell on some prosaic everyday detail in order to make his fictions more plausible, so the Mannerist painters of the sixteenth century often inserted some scrupulously exact still life into their otherwise highly patterned figure compositions. Clouet's meticulous rendition of the surfaces of fruits, bowl, and cloth in the 'Diane de Poitiers' is very different from his generalized painting of flesh in the adjacent half-length. He has not been satisfied with emphasizing the light and color of an 'optical' effect, as his successors Kalf and Drouais were to be (Pls. 124, 128). Combining his knowledge of the objects with his observation, Clouet has given a careful and incisive recording. Thus the still life acquires a high objectivity and an appearance of permanence that reinforces the formal order of the picture as a whole.

STILL LIFE
(DETAIL FROM GROUP PORTRAIT, FIG. 18)
Dated 1756. By François-Hubert Drouais (French)

THE abundant representation of still life in eighteenth-century French paintings is commonly a decorative accessory. Yet in a sense it belongs to their true theme, for the style of the period, called Rococo, is primarily decorative, and the figures, with their bright faces, powdered curls, and beribboned gowns, are like clusters of flowers. Whatever the subject, the effect is closely akin to that of a still life. In the play of light and shade, like the dancing of shadows over a sunlit lawn, and in the evanescent daintiness of ribbons and silken tissues, this box of finery expresses as clearly as the whole large picture from which it comes the glitter of society under Louis XV.

STILL LIFE (DETAIL FROM THE KITCHEN MAID, PL. 117)
Dated 1738. By Chardin (French)

A DMITTED to membership in the French Academy with the un-precedented title of still-life and genre painter, Chardin is the first of the distinguished line of French artists who have chosen to make the painting of still life a major consideration. Even when his still life is included in a figure composition its significance is not contingent. What makes this tiny painting of utensils monumental is the artist's complete realization of their existence, both individual and typical. Looking at the picture, one has the impression of grasping for the first time the intrinsic quality of a crock and the beauty of light reflected on old copper.

VASE OF FLOWERS
About 1875. By Cézanne (French)

CÉZANNE was no less devoted than Chardin to expressing the existence of things. His long, stubborn efforts to this end taxed his human models almost beyond endurance and made flowers a rare subject among his still lifes. Yet Cézanne's paintings excel in vitality. 'Still life' seems a misnomer for these flowers that shoot out on firm stems or bend gracefully as if fanned by a breeze. Even the elaborate blue scroll decoration of the bizarre vase joins in the joyous harmony of movement and color.

LANDSCAPE WITH A CITY (DETAIL FROM THE NATIVITY, FIG. 3)
About 1445. By Petrus Christus (Flemish)

DID one of the van Eycks paint 'the first modern landscapes,' those precious miniatures in the Hours of Turin? Was Petrus Christus really a pupil in the van Eyck studio? Affirmative answers to these disputed questions would help account for the unexpected magic of this landscape, the gentle dawn breaking on the horizon, the distant hills rising in the mist, the miniaturelike treatment of details. Through the magnifying glass the landscape is a treasure-trove. We try to identify the plants, and we search for insects among the flowers; and then our eye is led away to roam over distant hills and valleys. Though no heed is paid to our laws of perspective, we easily find our way through the vast expanse.

LANDSCAPE WITH A CASTLE (DETAIL FROM ST. VERONICA)
About 1470. By Memling (Flemish)

To Memling, a much younger fellow-townsman of Petrus Christus, landscape was no longer an exciting field of discovery, nor did he lose himself in its every detail. Here there is nothing of Petrus Christus' attempt to show nature's unexpected effects, with trees spaced in haphazard fashion or hills cutting across a town in a valley. In Memling's conception landscape is a serene, tranquil setting for figures, whether in religious subjects or portraiture. So he arranges his grassy meadows, quiet lakes, rippling streams, shapely trees, and distant castles in orderly, graceful patterns, and bathes them all in silvery light. Memling is the Perugino of Flemish art (see Pl. 23).

LANDSCAPE IN THE VENETO
(DETAIL FROM THE ADORATION OF THE SHEPHERDS)
About 1510. By Giorgione (Venetian)

WHETHER or not he ever painted independent landscapes, Giorgione, following the lead of his master Bellini, caught in such backgrounds as this the essence of idyllic landscape. Though the terrain, the buildings, and the golden light belong more specifically to the neighborhood of Venice, the mood of quiet dreaminess is peculiar to no one place or time. Nearly half a millennium later and in another clime we respond to every phase of Giorgione's feeling. So would an Oriental. Time and again in Giorgione we are reminded of those precious Sung paintings on silk that bring us into communion with Chinese masters of a thousand years ago. Titian, working beside Giorgione, soon began to strike out toward something more robust. Indeed he may well be the one who increased the density of the trees and shrubbery in this painting.

MOUNTAIN LANDSCAPE
(DETAIL FROM BELLINI'S FEAST OF THE GODS, PL. 45)
About 1520. By Titian (Venetian)

A FEW years after Bellini had signed his great painting of the Feast of the Gods, Titian, presumably to harmonize the picture with his own decorations for the same room in the Este castle at Ferrara, painted this towering crag over the left half of Bellini's frieze of trees. Titian's inspiration was no doubt the scenery of his birthplace, the rugged district of Cadore. And with the bold, jagged outlines of his native mountains he proclaims the course of the long career ahead of him. Already he reaches out from the quiet forms of his early associate, Giorgione, toward the heroic proportions and dramatic movement of the Late Renaissance. Satyrs, descried here among the trees, goat-footed creatures of Classical mythology, bring Titian's modern landscape into keeping with Bellini's ancient theme.

LANDSCAPE WITH FIGURES
Dated 1544. By Hirschvogel (German)

THE sixteenth century saw a great upsurge of landscape art in Germany, although there as elsewhere landscape was used chiefly as setting for figure subjects and seldom appears independently except in such drawings as this. What distinguishes German landscapes from others of the period is their eerie, almost fearsome character, a consequence, perhaps, of the dangers encountered or imagined in the deep German forests and mountain wilds. Even in this open, sunny view by Hirschvogel, where small fields are safely fenced in, and untroubled fishermen ply their task, one half expects some weird forest creature to peer out from the gnarled trees, with their queer weeping foliage. In the middle distance the horrid, bare crag shooting up mysteriously from the fields makes one grateful for the slender bridge that leads from its base to the fastness of the castle beyond.

THE TEMPTATION OF ST. ANTHONY
About 1555. By Pieter Bruegel the Elder (Flemish)

H IRSCHVOGEL'S Flemish contemporary Bruegel painted the most
modern landscapes of any before the seventeenth century. In this
landscape with the Temptation of St. Anthony all the monstrous
creatures of the imagination that Bruegel (under the influence of Bosch)
has been able to conjure up cannot detract from his sensitive appreciation of the slender leafy trees, of the warm sunlight falling into the little
clearing, and of the luminous stretch of water under the radiant clouds.
The real subject of the painting is the landscape. The strange riders in
the sky are scarcely more conspicuous than birds; and all the other
weird beings blend with the earth and foliage. It takes some searching to
find St. Anthony, who sits patiently under his poor shelter as unper-
turbed as the great landscape itself by all the little tormenters.

EXOTIC LANDSCAPE (DETAIL FROM THE REST
ON THE FLIGHT INTO EGYPT, FIG. 5)
About 1530. By Scorel (Dutch)

S COREL not only spent several years of study in Italy; he traveled also
to the Holy Land before coming home to Holland. Perhaps seeing
so many and so varied sights was partly responsible for the extravagance
of his landscape. The luminous atmospheric effect in paintings like this
might have made him a harbinger of the great seventeenth-century
Dutch landscapists. But in his effort to suggest movement and to give
an impression of the exotic scenery of his travels he has twisted plant
forms into such unusual shapes and forced his beautiful luminosity into
such fantastic patterns that, far from predicting the simplicity and
naturalism of his seventeenth-century descendants, he appears here as a
thorough-going Mannerist.

VIEW OF TOLEDO (DETAIL FROM ST. MARTIN AND
THE BEGGAR, PL. 36)
1597/99. By El Greco (Spanish)

BENEATH the raised hoof of St. Martin's white horse we get only a glimpse of El Greco's beloved Toledo. But it is enough to suggest the majestic beauty possible in a Mannerist landscape. El Greco never seems, like Scorel, to strive for an effect but, rather, to follow an inner compulsion. It is the *spirit* of Toledo that he has painted here. The brilliant cloud brushed across the sky, the luminous towers pointing upward like nervous fingers, the silver light running along the distant ridges, the glowing spray on the great water wheel—all this is a visible counterpart to the mysticism and religious fervor that fired Toledo in El Greco's day.

LANDSCAPE WITH BOY FISHING

About 1515. By Domenico Campagnola (Venetian)

WE have a few landscape drawings, complete in themselves, by Titian and Giorgione. But it is one of Titian's pupils, Domenico Campagnola, who seems to have been more specifically a landscapist. In 1537 Michiel wrote that a collector in Padua had, besides large landscapes in tempera on canvas by this artist, other ones drawn in pen and ink on paper. Today this delightful little pen-and-ink landscape is almost the only drawing unanimously accepted as Campagnola's. One wonders how much in it is due to the influence of Titian and Giorgione, who delighted in such picturesque buildings and hilly terrain, and how much Campagnola won from the study of actual views. The slight weight and doubtful substance of things does not suggest very searching observation. Yet Campagnola's drawings, or those associated with his name, have always been highly prized, and we are not surprised to find that Watteau, for example, was strongly attracted by their poetic mood and copied all he found in the great Crozat Collection.

LANDSCAPE WITH COTTAGE AND HAY BARN
About 1650. By Rembrandt (Dutch)

ONE does not question Rembrandt's intimacy with nature as one does Campagnola's. There is no special theme in this small drawing, no attempt to make it picturesque or poetic. It shows merely a group of low thatched buildings beside a pond and a road, and beyond, at the left, the flat country stretching to the horizon. One would soon finish counting the number of times Rembrandt's pen touched the paper. But never could one duplicate those touches or rub onto the paper, as he has done, the light washes of ink to give such a sense of the atmosphere and of the play of light and shadow. Beyond the technical skill, there is the master's superior power of observation and his devotion to visible things. These buildings and all their surroundings live for us, not through any sentimental suggestion but through the rightness of each detail and its perfect adjustment to the whole. Rembrandt's drawings, like Campagnola's were highly valued. His younger contemporary Zoomer, an Amsterdam art dealer, put his mark, as owner, at the lower left of this drawing; and the initials of William Esdaile, the eighteenth-century English banker and collector of fine prints and drawings, are at the right.

LANDSCAPE

About 1600. By Annibale Carracci (Bolognese)

S OME wish to see in the eclectic Annibale Carracci the founder of pure landscape painting in Italy, and it is not unusual to find, as here, nearly the whole of his canvas given over to trees, lakes, and mountains. But he still conceives of landscape as something primarily decorative, a kind of theatrical scene painting. Details of this picture are not very convincing as studies from nature. They look secondhand, as if they had been taken from such an artist as Tintoretto, then put together as one moves in coulisses at either side of a stage. Why it is that, though excellent decoration, this is not pure landscape painting, becomes evident when we see it beside a picture by Claude Lorrain. Carracci lacked, above all, Claude's unifying light.

THE HERDSMAN
About 1655/60. By Claude Lorrain (French)

CARRACCI could never have anticipated Claude's light effects because he did not have Claude's enthusiasm for nature. In this scene, stretching from pastoral foreground to distant mountains, we sense his exaltation. He is still far from the chance effects of nineteenth-century Impressionism. Claude *arranged* his compositions, and he indulged his poetic mood. But his devotion to light, especially to the golden light of the veiled sun as it sinks toward the Italian horizon, made his pictures so convincing that even today our vision of nature is not a little determined by Claude's vision.

FOREST SCENE
About 1660/65. By Jacob van Ruisdael (Dutch)

I N any survey of landscape painting we should give much attention to
the seventeenth-century Dutch artists. Hardly one of them but
painted out-of-door scenes on occasion; and for nearly two centuries
this was the school to which every young landscapist, in England at
least, looked for inspiration. Ruisdael was the most emotional of the
Dutchmen who concentrated on landscape. Here we see him in a sombre
mood. The small figures in the distance seem swallowed up in all this
irrepressible growth and inevitable decay.

LANDSCAPE WITH A BRIDGE
About 1785. By Gainsborough (British)

THIS decorative landscape, which was painted near the end of Gainsborough's life, gives little hint that his early inspiration came from Ruisdael and that he actually made copies after that meticulous Dutchman. However, the lesson was never forgotten. Even when Gainsborough had developed his own feathery technique, painting with brushes six feet long from a palette dripping with liquid pigments, he kept Ruisdael's clear, just relationship between earth, air, and trees. He did not reflect Ruisdael's sombre mood. In this painting the people are small but not oppressed by the landscape, and a snug cottage awaits them in the shelter of the cliff.

145

HORSEMEN AND HERDSMEN WITH CATTLE
About 1660/70. By Aelbert Cuyp (Dutch)

THE late afternoon was Cuyp's favorite time of day. He has studied this broad stretch of scenery with the western sky almost directly in front of him. The beams of the low sun fill all the air with a golden haze, veil the distant prospect of land and water, and throw long shadows across the foreground. Cuyp's all-pervading light recalls his French contemporary Claude Lorrain (see Pl. 142). But the special glory of Cuyp is his sky, its vast space measured by banks of slowly moving clouds. This is a lesson in sky effect that was to be well conned by early nineteenth-century British landscapists.

WIVENHOE PARK, ESSEX
1816. By Constable (British)

IT was not enough for Constable to paint great cumulus clouds racing
each other across the sky, all the sky he could get on his canvas. On
the ground and on the water he recorded the play of shadows cast by
other clouds passing low above him. We know from his correspondence
that he was long in finishing this painting of Wivenhoe Park, that the
extent of view required by the owner of the estate made the task
difficult. Yet the picture retains much of the freshness and spontaneity
of the sketches that the artist used to dash off rapidly and date with the
hour, as well as the day and the month. It is his consciousness of
nature's swift changing that distinguishes Constable most sharply from
his Dutch predecessors and links him with his Impressionist descendants.

THE MILL
About 1650. By Rembrandt (Dutch)

LIKE its majestic mill rising high against the sunset sky, this painting
stands in solitary greatness. It has no close parallel in Rembrandt's
works, or even in the whole range of landscape painting. That Rembrandt's vast output includes comparatively few landscapes is of no
special significance. One subject as well as another becomes sublime
under the touch of his all-embracing sympathy. The perfect balance
here of actuality and poetry bespeaks an artist of highest intellectual and
deepest spiritual capacity.

KEELMEN HEAVING IN COALS BY MOONLIGHT
Probably 1835. By Turner (British)

'MASTERS of the Black Arts,' Ruskin called the Dutch landscapists in opposition to critics who dubbed Turner and his followers 'White Painters.' Yet Turner was deeply impressed by the sombre majesty of Rembrandt's Mill. He copied it, and in his early paintings he repeated its contrasts. Only later the bright haze of Claude Lorrain, the sunshine of Venice, and his own brilliant watercolor technique, emulated in oil, sped on his pursuit of dazzling light. In this night scene moonlight and flame nearly fill the picture, and poetry threatens to crowd out actuality.

THE SWING
About 1765. By Fragonard (French)

WHEN Fragonard painted this large canvas he had returned from an enchanting sojourn at the Villa d'Este, that estate of fabulous gardens overlooking the Campagna east of Rome. His memory and his sketchbook were filled with the vistas and distant prospects that had held him spellbound. The graceful figures he loved to paint are here of little importance as people; they are like bouquets of bright flowers scattered over the terrace. The landscape is the theme—great feathery trees, sun-touched mountains, and banks of fleecy clouds. There is nothing ominous in the vastness. This is a decorative landscape, with the pure, delicate colors and studied casualness of design that are the delight of a Rococo masterpiece.

MADAME MONET UNDER THE WILLOWS
Dated 1880. By Monet (French)

WHAT a difference a century made in the French conception of landscape painting! The picturesque scenery of Tivoli was very important to Fragonard. Monet could content himself with a few scraggly trees (by chance his wife sits among them here), so long as he had the swiftly changing light of day to clothe them with its magic. This was scenery enough for as many paintings as there were variations in light through the day and through the seasons. To catch any one light effect, Monet had to paint rapidly, with broad, sketchy strokes, and he had to leave to our eyes the matter of fusing the fresh, vibrating colors that are the life of an Impressionist masterpiece.

A VIEW NEAR VOLTERRA
Dated 1838. By Corot (French)

I T would be interesting to inquire why Italy was so important in the
development of French landscape painting. Only there did Poussin
and Claude, in the seventeenth century, find their highest expression.
Only there did Fragonard ripen, in the eighteenth century. And only
there was Corot at his best, in the nineteenth. Probably the actual
Italian scenery was less responsible than was a sense of nearness to
Classical antiquity, that great inculcator of selectivity. The forms in
Corot's Italian pictures, such as A View near Volterra, are blocked out
in bold planes that anticipate Cézanne. Corot's avowed purpose was to
hold on to his first impression and give a sincere report of it in his painting, without worrying about the effect. It was in Italy that he realized
his aim most fully.

THE LACKAWANNA VALLEY
1855. By Inness (American)

INNESS had visited Italy twice before he painted this picture. But lacking the foundation of Latin culture, which Frenchmen are all but born with, he does not give much evidence of having learned the Classical lesson of selection and simplification. The descriptive conception of landscape painting revealed in this panorama of the Lackawanna Valley was inherited from the Hudson River School. But Inness had one thing in common with Corot, a simple love of nature that gave a ring of sincerity to his work. Even this picture, burdened as it is with the detail demanded by the railroad company that commissioned it, is unified by the mood of serenity which the broad views of his native country seem to have inspired in Inness.

GARDEN OF PARADISE (DETAIL FROM THE ANNUNCIATION, FIG. 19)

About 1445. By Giovanni di Paolo (Sienese)

A THOROUGH training in the expert technical methods of his day and a generous inheritance of the best traditions of his past equipped Giovanni di Paolo for some of the most sophisticated painting the Early Renaissance has left to us. Yet when he wished to paint something so completely unknown as Paradise, he went into his own little garden and sketched the graceful violets, the sprightly daisies, the lacy pinks, the ripening strawberries, and among them the long-eared rabbits at play. Plants and animals are drawn with a sensitive appreciation of the various species; but they are arranged one above another, as on a tapestry. This is the terrain over which Adam and Eve hasten before the minatory hand of God's messenger.

THE EQUATORIAL JUNGLE
Dated 1909. By Henri Rousseau (French)

R OUSSEAU was self-taught. He knew very little about traditional techniques and traditional theories of art. Yet when he thought to represent what he saw daily in the botanical and zoological gardens, he seems to have delved into his subconscious past and to have been obsessed by some primeval conception. He studied the plants and animals with passionate interest and then came home to paint the patterns into which his imagination had transformed what he had seen. The stylized design of each plant and animal, although it contrasts as sharply as possible with Giovanni di Paolo's naturalistic flowers and rabbits, is woven into a composition that parallels the tapestry effect of Giovanni's Garden of Paradise.

LANDSCAPE IN PROVENCE
1878/83. By Cézanne (French)

A TYPICAL Impressionist's preoccupation with momentary light effects tended to disintegrate design and form. Cézanne, on the contrary, saw nature in terms of pattern and volume. This gave his composition a kind of Classical orderliness, which was pushed by his followers to the extreme of Cubism. One understands why Cézanne, with his eye for volume, chose this view, where buildings play a prominent rôle. To realize their three-dimensional character he emphasized their angles, not so much by line as by the use of contrasting colors on adjoining planes.

THE OLIVE ORCHARD
1889. By Van Gogh (Dutch)

A TYPICAL Impressionist took care to exclude emotion from his visual impression. But Van Gogh's seeing and his attempt to record what he saw involved his whole being, so that his paintings are emotional expressions rather than visual impressions. Yet no one was ever more earnest in his study of nature. These olive trees, with their twisting trunks and boughs and darting foliage, are vividly alive. All is fierce tension and movement here, while all is harmonious composure in Cézanne's Landscape in Provence.

S. MARIA DELLA FEBBRE, ROME
Dated 1629. By Saenredam (Dutch)

PAINTINGS of architecture and city views are akin to landscape not so much through the presence and frequent importance of terrain and sky as through a common emphasis on effects of light. We associate emphasis on light with the Impressionists. Yet two centuries before their time Saenredam left exquisite paintings of light effects, using architectural views, usually interiors, as vehicles for his light. The landscape settings of his rare exteriors were sometimes painted by collaborators, as may have been the case in this Roman view. Sometimes he had not even seen the architecture he painted. This view of S. Maria della Febbre—Saenredam never visited Rome—was taken from a drawing he owned by Marten van Heemskerck. But in Saenredam's interpretation the building has gained remarkably in depth and clarity. As usual, he keeps the coloring in a high key, and the rich composition of recessions and projections depends on the subtlest play of soft, clear light and luminous shadows. A very personal art, Saenredam's work eschews fanfare and eludes imitators.

VIEW IN VENICE
About 1740. By Canaletto (Venetian)

CANALETTO'S talent alone might have been enough to make city views popular in the eighteenth century. But the enthusiasm of British tourists also contributed. They had 'discovered' the poetic charm of Venice, and they bought Canaletto's views as souvenirs. Back home they began to see some reminiscence of Venetian charm in their own London, and they sent for Canaletto to interpret it. Even today certain views in London, but especially views in Venice, are closely associated in our minds with Canaletto. When we stand in the Piazza SS. Giovanni e Paolo, shown in this picture, the sparkling light on the buildings and the reflections in the water are enhanced for us because our vision has been conditioned by such paintings as this. Canaletto's style is more brilliant than Saenredam's and less subtle in its means of expression. Connoisseurs must beware of its many imitators.

CAMPO S. ZANIPOLO
1782. By Guardi (Venetian)

G UARDI, like Canaletto, enjoyed British patronage. This view of the Piazza SS. Giovanni e Paolo ('Campo S. Zanipolo' in Venetian dialect) is a study for a painting commissioned by a British resident in Venice. The final composition, one version of which is now in Oxford, represents Pope Pius VI pronouncing a benediction in the piazza on May 19, 1782. Guardi received his commission two days after the event, and this study of the temporary stairway and papal balcony, which had been built against the façade of the Scuola di S. Marco for the ceremony, shows the piazza taken over by the curious. They climb up and down the stairway, so lately barred to them, and they crowd onto the balcony, where the pope stood. Comparison of Guardi's study with Canaletto's view of the same piazza, in Pl. 158, shows how much richer Guardi's brushwork is. His brilliant interpretation of the transforming effect of light is prophetic of the Impressionists.

HOUSE OF PÈRE LACROIX
Dated 1873. By Cézanne (French)

G UARDI uses his brilliant brushwork to produce a delicate effect, and the architecture in his Campo S. Zanipolo seems fragile and evanescent when compared with Cézanne's massive House of Père Lacroix. Guardi's painting is decorative, its tiny points of high light sparkling like a mass of jewels. Cézanne's is monumental, the broad planes of roofs and walls defining the bulk of the building. As we have already seen (Pl. 155), Cézanne, unlike the Impressionists of his day, uses light and color to emphasize the cubic content of his forms. Yet even as mere pattern his composition is extremely effective. The broad spotting of branches and foliage on this canvas is as seemingly casual as a shower of cherry blossoms painted on a Japanese screen.

INDEX

Unless otherwise indicated, the works indexed are in the National Gallery of Art, its collections being noted in parentheses.

ADRIAEN DE VRIES (About 1560–1627)

Virtue and Vice. Bronze. 30½ in. high. (*Widener Collection*). Pl.54

AGOSTINO DI DUCCIO (1418–shortly after 1480)

Madonna and Child. Marble. 28 × 22¾ in. (*Mellon Collection*). Pl.11

ALBERTI, LEON BATTISTA (1404–1472)

Self-Portrait. Bronze. 7⅞ × 5⅜ in. (*Samuel H. Kress Collection*). Pl.56

ANDREA DEL SARTO (1486–1531)

Charity. Panel. 47¼ × 36½ in. (*Samuel H. Kress Collection.*) Pl.52

ANGELICO, FRA (1387–1455) and FRA FILIPPO LIPPI (About 1406–1469)

The Adoration of the Magi. Panel. Diam. 54 in. (*Samuel H. Kress Collection*). Pls.9, 106

ANTONELLO DA MESSINA (1430–1479)

Portrait of a Young Man. Panel. 13 × 9¾ in. (*Mellon Collection*). Pl.63

BAROCCI, FEDERICO (1535–1612)

Quintilia Fischieri. Canvas. 48¾ × 37½ in. (*Samuel H. Kress Collection*). Pl.81

BELLINI, GIOVANNI (About 1430–1516)

Madonna and Child. Panel 28¼ × 20⅞ in. (*Ralph and Mary Booth Collection*). Pl.29

Orpheus. Canvas. 18⅝ × 32 in. (*Widener Collection*). Pl.43

Portrait of a Young Man in Red. Panel. 12½ × 10⅜ in. (*Mellon Collection*). Pl.64

The Feast of the Gods. Canvas. 67 × 74 in. (*Widener Collection*). Pls.45, 134

BENEDETTO DA MAIANO (1442–1497)

Bust of a Florentine Statesman. Terra-cotta. 22½ in. high. (*Samuel H. Kress Collection*). Fig.14

BERNINI, LORENZO (1598–1680)

Louis XIV. Bronze. 33⅛ in. high. (*Samuel H. Kress Collection*). Pl.84

BLAKE, WILLIAM (1757–1827)

The Woman Clothed with the Sun. Watercolor on paper. 16 × 13 in. (*Rosenwald Collection*). Pl.22

BOLTRAFFIO, GIOVANNI ANTONIO (1467–1516)

Portrait of a Youth. Panel. 18¾ × 13¾ in. (*Ralph and Mary Booth Collection*). Pl.69

BOSCH, HIERONYMUS (About 1450–1516)

Death and the Miser. Panel. 36⅝ × 12¼ in. (*Samuel H. Kress Collection*). Pl.53

BOTTICELLI (1444–1510)

Giuliano de' Medici. Panel. 29¾ × 20⅝ in. (*Samuel H. Kress Collection*). Pl.62

The Adoration of the Magi. Panel. 27⅝ × 41 in. (*Mellon Collection*). Pl.31

BOUCHER, FRANÇOIS (1703–1770)

Allegory of Music. Canvas. 40¾ × 51⅛ in. (*Samuel H. Kress Collection*). Pl.49

Madame Bergeret. Canvas. 56¼ × 41¾ in. (*Samuel H. Kress Collection*). Pl.95

BRONZINO, AGNOLO (1503–1572)

A Young Woman and Her Little Boy. Panel. 39¼ × 29⅞ in. (*Widener Collection*). Fig.17; Pl.71

BRUEGEL, PIETER THE ELDER (About 1525–1569)

The Temptation of St. Anthony. Panel. 23 × 33¾ in. (*Samuel H. Kress Collection*). Pl.136

BURGUNDIAN (?), About 1400

Morse representing the Trinity. Gold and Enamel. Diam. 5 in. (*Widener Collection*). Pl.8

BYZANTINE, XIII Century

Enthroned Madonna and Child. Canvas on panel. 51⅝ × 30¼ in. (*Gift of Mrs. Otto H. Kahn*). Pl.2

CAMPAGNOLA, DOMENICO (1500–after 1552)

Landscape with Boy Fishing. Drawing on paper. 6½ × 9¾ in. (*Rosenwald Collection*). Pl.139

CANALETTO (1697–1768)

View in Venice. Canvas. 28 × 44 in. (*Widener Collection*). Pl.158

CARAVAGGIO (1573–1610)

Still Life. Canvas. 19⅞ × 28¼ in. (*Samuel H. Kress Collection*). Pl.125

CARPACCIO, VITTORE (About 1455–1523/26)

Madonna and Child. Panel. 33⅜ × 26⅞ in. (*Samuel H. Kress Collection*). Pl.33

CARRACCI, ANNIBALE (1560–1609)

Landscape. Canvas. 34¾ × 58¼ in. (*Samuel H. Kress Collection*). Pl.141

CASTAGNO, ANDREA DEL (1423–1457)

Portrait of a Man. Panel. 21¼ × 15⅞ in. (*Mellon Collection*). Pl.61
The Youthful David. Leather on wood. 45½ × 30¼ (16⅛ at bottom) in. (*Widener Collection*). Pl.17

CÉZANNE, PAUL (1839–1906)

House of Père Lacroix. Canvas. 24¼ × 20 in. (*Chester Dale Collection*). Pl.160
Landscape in Provence. Canvas. 19¾ × 23⅞ in. (*Chester Dale Collection*). Pl. 155
Vase of Flowers. Canvas. 28¾ × 23½ in. (*Chester Dale Collection*). Pl.130

CHARDIN, JEAN-BAPTISTE-SIMÉON (1699–1779)

The House of Cards. Canvas. 32⅜ × 26 in. (*Mellon Collection*). Pl.116
The Kitchen Maid. Canvas. 18⅛ × 14¾ in. (*Samuel H. Kress Collection*). Pls.117,129

CHRISTUS, PETRUS (About 1410–1472/73)

A Donor and His Wife. Panel. Each 16½ × 8½ in. (*Samuel H. Kress Collection.*). Pl.58
The Nativity. Panel. 51¼ × 38¼ in. (*Mellon Collection*). Fig.3; Pls.105, 131

CLAUDE LORRAIN (1600–1682)

The Herdsman. Canvas. 47¾ × 63⅛ in. (*Samuel H. Kress Collection*). Pl.142

CLOUET, FRANÇOIS (About 1510–1572)

'Diane de Poitiers.' Panel. 36¼ × 32 in. (*Samuel H. Kress Collection*). Frontispiece; Pl.127

CONSTABLE, JOHN (1776–1837)

Wivenhoe Park. Canvas. 22 × 39¾ in. (*Widener Collection*). Pl.146

235

COROT, JEAN-BAPTISTE-CAMILLE (1796–1875)
A View near Volterra. Canvas. 27⅜ × 37½ in. (*Chester Dale Collection*).
Pl.151

COSSA, FRANCESCO DEL (About 1435–1477)
The Crucifixion. Panel. 25⅛ × 24⅞ in. (*Samuel H.Kress Collection*). Pl.10

CRIVELLI, CARLO (1430/35–after 1493)
Madonna and Child. Panel. 15½ × 12 in. (*Samuel H. Kress Collection*).
Pl.12

CUYP, AELBERT (1620–1691)
Horsemen and Herdsmen with Cattle. Canvas. 47⅜ × 67 in. (*Widener Collection*). Pl.145

DAUMIER, HONORÉ (1808–1879)
Advice to a Young Artist. Canvas. 16⅛ × 12⅞ in. (*Gift of Duncan Phillips*). Pl.118

DAVID, GERARD (About 1460–1523)
The Rest on the Flight into Egypt. Panel. 17¾ × 17½ in. (*Mellon Collection*). Pl.25

DAVID, JACQUES-LOUIS (1748–1825)
Madame David. Canvas. 28¾ × 23¼ in. (*Samuel H. Kress Collection*).
Pl.97
Napoleon in His Study. Canvas. 80¼ × 49¼ in. (*Samuel H. Kress Collection*). Pl.96

DEGAS, EDGAR (1834–1917)
The Duke and Duchess of Morbilli. Canvas. 46¼ × 35½ in. (*Chester Dale Collection*). Pl.100

DESIDERIO DA SETTIGNANO (1428–1464)
St. Jerome in the Desert. Marble. 16¾ × 21½ in. (*Widener Collection*).
Pl.19
The Christ Child. Marble. 12 in. high. (*Samuel H. Kress Collection*).
Pl.93

DONATELLO (About 1386–1466)
The David of the Casa Martelli. Marble. 64¾ in. high. (*Widener Collection*). Pl.18

DOSSI, DOSSO (About 1479–1542)
Circe and Her Lovers in a Landscape. Canvas. 39⅝ × 53½ in. (*Samuel H. Kress Collection*). Pl.44

DROUAIS, FRANÇOIS-HUBERT (1727–1775)
Group Portrait. Canvas. 96×76⅝ in. (*Samuel H. Kress Collection*).
Fig.18; Pl.128

DUCCIO (1278–not later than 1318)
The Nativity. Panel. 17¼×17½ in. (*Mellon Collection*). Pl.5

DÜRER, ALBRECHT (1471–1528)
Madonna and Child. Panel. 20¾×16⅞ in. (*Samuel H. Kress Collection*).
Pl.30
Portrait of a Clergyman. Parchment on canvas. 17×13 in. (*Samuel H.
Kress Collection*). Pl.70
St. Eustace. Engraving. 14×10⅛ in. (*Rosenwald Collection*). Pl.27

DYCK, SIR ANTHONY VAN (1599–1641)
Marchesa Elena Grimaldi, Wife of Marchese Nicola Cattaneo. Canvas.
97×68 in. (*Widener Collection*). Pl.87
Paola Adorno, Marchesa Brignole Sale, and Her Son. Canvas.
74½×55 in. (*Widener Collection*). Pl.82

EARLY CHRISTIAN, V Century
The Good Shepherd. Mosaic. Mausoleum of Galla Placidia, *Ravenna*.
Fig.20

EYCK, JAN VAN (1380/1400–1441)
The Annunciation. Transferred from wood to canvas. 36½×14⅜ in.
(*Mellon Collection*). Fig.6; Pls.7,121

EYCK, HUBERT VAN (Active first half XV Century)
and JAN VAN EYCK (1380/1400–1441)
Details from the Ghent Altarpiece. St. Bavon, *Ghent*. Figs.13,22,23

FALCONET, ÉTIENNE-MAURICE (1716–1791)
Venus of the Doves. Marble. 29½ in. high. (*Samuel H. Kress Collection*).
Pl.48

FLORENTINE, Late XIII Century
Madonna and Child with Saints. Birmingham Museum of Art, Samuel
H. Kress Collection, *Birmingham, Alabama*. Fig.2

FRAGONARD, JEAN-HONORÉ (1732–1806)
Blindman's Buff. Canvas. 85⅛×77⅞ in. (*Samuel H. Kress Collection*).
Pl.120
The Swing. Canvas. 85×73 in. (*Samuel H. Kress Collection*). Pl.149

237

FRANCO-FLEMISH, About 1390/1400

The Death of the Virgin. Silverpoint on paper prepared with terra-verde ground. 11⅜ × 15⅞ in. (*Rosenwald Collection*). Pl.6

FRANCO-FLEMISH, 1402

Marcia Painting Her Self-Portrait (from the 'Boccace de Philippe le Hardi.' Bibliothèque Nationale, *Paris*. Fig.12

FRANCO-FLEMISH (Pol de Limbourg ?), About 1410

Portrait of a Lady. Panel. 20⅜ × 14⅜ in. (*Mellon Collection*). Pl.55

FRENCH, About 1140

The Chalice of Abbot Suger. Silver gilt, precious stones and jewels. 7½ in. high. (*Widener Collection*). Pl.1

GAINSBOROUGH, THOMAS (1727–1788)

Georgiana, Duchess of Devonshire. Canvas. 92½ × 57½ in. (*Mellon Collection*). Pl.89
Landscape with a Bridge. Canvas. 44½ × 52½ in. (*Mellon Collection*). Pl.144

GENTILE DA FABRIANO (About 1360–1427)

Madonna and Child. Panel. 37¾ × 22¼ in. (*Samuel H. Kress Collection*). Pl.4

GIORGIONE (About 1478–1510)

The Adoration of the Shepherds. Panel. 35¾ × 43½ in. (*Samuel H. Kress Collection*). Pl.133
The Holy Family. Panel. 14⅝ × 17⅞ in. (*Samuel H. Kress Collection*). Pl.32

GIOVANNI DI PAOLO (1403–1482)

The Adoration of the Magi. Panel. 10¼ × 17¾ in. (*Mellon Collection*). Fig.24
The Annunciation. Panel. 15¾ × 18¼ in. (*Samuel H. Kress Collection*). Fig.19; Pl.153

GOGH, VINCENT VAN (1853–1890)

La Mousmé. Canvas. 28¾ × 23¾ in. (*Chester Dale Collection*). Pl.102
The Olive Orchard. Canvas. 28¾ × 36¼ in. (*Chester Dale Collection*). Pl.156

GOSSAERT, JAN (Mabuse) (About 1478–1533/36)

St. Jerome Penitent. Panel. Each, 34 × 10 in. (*Samuel H. Kress Collection*). Pl.20

238

Goya, Francisco de (1746–1828)

Marquesa de Pontejos. Canvas. 83 × 49¾ in. (*Mellon Collection*). Pl.90

Gozzoli, Benozzo (1420–1497)

The Dance of Salome. Panel. 9⅜ × 13½ in. (*Samuel H. Kress Collection*). Pl.16

Greco, El (Dominico Theotocópuli) (1541–1614)

Christ Cleansing the Temple. Panel. 25¾ × 32¾ in. (*Samuel H. Kress Collection*). Pl.38

Laocoön. Canvas. 54⅛ × 68 in. (*Samuel H. Kress Collection*). Pl.46

St. Martin and the Beggar. Canvas. 76⅛ × 40½ in. (*Widener Collection*). Pls.36, 138

Greuze, Jean-Baptiste (1725–1805)

Monsieur de la Live de Jully. Canvas. 46 × 34⅞ in. (*Samuel H. Kress Collection*). Pl. 86

Grünewald (Mathis Gothart Nithart) (About 1465–1528)

The Small Crucifixion. Panel. 24¼ × 18⅛ in. (*Samuel H. Kress Collection*). Pl.24

Guardi, Francesco (1712–1793)

Campo S. Zanipolo. Canvas. 14¾ × 12⅜ in. (*Samuel H. Kress Collection*). Pl.159

Hals, Frans (About 1580–1666)

Portrait of an Elderly Lady. Canvas. 40½ × 34 in. (*Mellon Collection*). Pl.101

Hamen y Leon, Juan van der (1596–1631)

Still Life. Canvas. 33 × 44½ in. (*Samuel H. Kress Collection*). Pl.126

Hirschvogel, Augustin (1503–1553)

Landscape with Figures. Drawing on paper. 5¾ × 9 in. (*Rosenwald Collection*). Pl.135

Holbein, Hans the Younger (1497–1543)

Edward VI as a Child. Panel. 22⅜ × 17⅜ in. (*Mellon Collection*). Pl.72

Hooch, Pieter de (1629–about 1683)

A Dutch Courtyard. Canvas. 26¾ × 23 in. (*Mellon Collection*). Pl.112

Houdon, Jean-Antoine (1741–1828)

Alexandre Brongniard. Marble. 15⅜ in. high. (*Widener Collection*). Pl.94

INGRES, JEAN-AUGUSTE-DOMINIQUE (1780–1867)
Madame Moitessier. Canvas. 58¼ × 40 in. (*Samuel H. Kress Collection*). Pl.98

INNESS, GEORGE (1825–1894)
The Lackawanna Valley. Canvas. 33⅞ × 50⅛ in. (*Gift of Mrs. Huttleston Rogers*). Pl.152

KALF, WILLEM (1622–1693)
Still Life. Canvas. 25⅜ × 21¼ in. (*Gift of Chester Dale*). Pl.124

LAURANA, FRANCESCO DA (About 1425–1502)
A Princess of the House of Aragon. Marble. 17½ in. high. (*Mellon Collection*). Pl.79

LE NAIN, LOUIS (About 1593–1648)
A French Interior. Canvas. 21⅞ × 25¾ in. (*Samuel H. Kress Collection*). Pl.109

LEONI, LEONE (1509–1590)
Emperor Charles V. Bronze. 43⅛ in. high. (*Samuel H. Kress Collection*). Fig.15

LIMBOURG, POL DE (Active early XV Century)
April (from 'Les Très Riches Heures du Duc de Berry'). Musée Condé, *Chantilly*. Fig.21

LIPPI, FRA FILIPPO (About 1406–1469)
St. Benedict Orders St. Maurus to the Rescue of St. Placidus. Panel. 16¾ × 28 in. (*Samuel H. Kress Collection*). Pl.15

LIPPI, FRA FILIPPO (About 1406–1469) and FRA ANGELICO (1387–1455)
The Adoration of the Magi. Panel. Diam. 54 in. (*Samuel H. Kress Collection*). Pls.9,106

LONGHI, PIETRO (1702–1785)
A Game of *Pignatta*. Canvas. 19¼ × 24 in. (*Samuel H. Kress Collection*). Pl.119

LORENZETTI, AMBROGIO (Active 1319–about 1348)
Madonna and Child Enthroned. S. Angelo a Vico l'Abate, *Florence*. Fig.4

LORENZO DI CREDI (About 1458–1537)
Self-Portrait. Transferred from wood to canvas. 18 × 12¾ in. (*Widener Collection*). Pl.77

LOTTO, LORENZO (About 1480–1556)

Allegory. Panel. $22\frac{1}{4} \times 17\frac{1}{8}$ in. (*Samuel H. Kress Collection*). Pl.51

LUCAS VAN LEYDEN (1494–1533)

The Card Players. Panel. $21\frac{3}{4} \times 23\frac{7}{8}$ in. (*Samuel H. Kress Collection*). Pls.107, 123

MANET, ÉDOUARD (1832–1883)

The Old Musician. Canvas. $73\frac{3}{4} \times 98$ in. (*Chester Dale Collection*). Pl.110

MARGARITONE (Mentioned 1262)

Madonna and Child Enthroned. Panel. $38\frac{1}{8} \times 19\frac{1}{2}$ in. (*Samuel H. Kress Collection*). Fig.1

MASTER OF THE FRANCISCAN CRUCIFIXES, About 1250

St. John the Evangelist. Panel. $31\frac{5}{8} \times 12\frac{1}{2}$ in. (*Samuel H. Kress Collection*). Pl.3

The Mourning Madonna. Panel. $31\frac{7}{8} \times 12\frac{3}{8}$ in. (*Samuel H. Kress Collection*). Pl.3

MASTER OF THE ST. LUCY LEGEND (Dated works 1480 and 1489)

Mary, Queen of Heaven. Panel. 85×73 in. (*Samuel H. Kress Collection*). Pl.21

MEMLING, HANS (About 1430/35–1494)

St. Veronica. Panel. $12\frac{1}{4} \times 9\frac{1}{2}$ in. (*Samuel H. Kress Collection*). Pl.132

The Chalice of St. John the Evangelist. Panel. $12\frac{1}{4} \times 9\frac{1}{2}$ in. (*Samuel H. Kress Collection*). Pl.122

MEMMI, LIPPO (Active 1317–1347)

Madonna and Child with Donor. Panel. $22\frac{1}{4} \times 9\frac{1}{2}$ in. (*Mellon Collection*). Fig.8

MONET, CLAUDE (1840–1926)

Madame Monet under the Willows. Canvas. $31\frac{7}{8} \times 23\frac{5}{8}$ in. (*Chester Dale Collection*). Pl.150

MORISOT, BERTHE (1841–1895)

The Mother and Sister of the Artist. Canvas. $39\frac{1}{2} \times 32$ in. (*Chester Dale Collection*). Pl.99

MORONI, GIOVANNI BATTISTA (1520/25–1578)

'Titian's Schoolmaster.' Canvas. $38\frac{1}{8} \times 29\frac{1}{4}$ in. (*Widener Collection*). Pl.74

Murillo, Bartolomé Esteban (1617–1682)

A Girl and Her Duenna. Canvas. $49\frac{3}{8} \times 41$ in. (*Widener Collection*). Pl.115

Nattier, Jean-Marc (1685–1766)

Joseph Bonnier de la Mosson. Canvas. $54\frac{1}{4} \times 41\frac{1}{2}$ in. (*Samuel H. Kress Collection*). Pl.85

Neroccio de' Landi (1447–1500)

Portrait of a Lady. Panel. $18\frac{3}{8} \times 12$ in. (*Widener Collection*). Pl.66

Perugino, Pietro (About 1445–1523)

The Crucifixion (middle panel of a triptych). Transferred from wood to canvas. $39\frac{7}{8} \times 22\frac{1}{4}$ in. (*Mellon Collection*). Pl.23

Pisanello (About 1395–1455)

Medal of Domenico Novello Malatesta. Bronze. Diam. $3\frac{3}{8}$ in. (*Samuel H. Kress Collection*). Fig.11

Medal of Filippo Maria Visconti. Bronze. Diam. $4\frac{1}{8}$ in. (*Samuel H. Kress Collection*). Fig.10

Medal of Leonello d'Este. Bronze. Diam. $4\frac{1}{8}$ in. (*Samuel H. Kress Collection*). Pl.57

Predis, Ambrogio de (About 1455–about 1508)

Bianca Maria Sforza. Panel. $20 \times 12\frac{3}{4}$ in. (*Widener Collection*). Pl. 65

Raeburn, Sir Henry (1756–1823)

Captain Patrick Miller. Canvas. $66 \times 52\frac{1}{4}$ in. (*Gift of Mrs. Dwight Davis*). Pl.92

Raphael (1483–1520)

St. George and the Dragon. Panel. $11\frac{1}{8} \times 8\frac{3}{8}$ in. (*Mellon Collection*). Pl.28

The Alba Madonna. Transferred from wood to canvas. Diam. $37\frac{1}{4}$ in. (*Mellon Collection*). Pl.26

The Small Cowper Madonna. Panel. $23\frac{3}{8} \times 17\frac{3}{8}$ in. (*Widener Collection*). Pl.34

Rembrandt van Ryn (1606–1669)

A Girl with a Broom. Canvas. $42\frac{1}{4} \times 36$ in. (*Mellon Collection*). Pl.113

Christ Healing the Sick. Etching. $10\frac{7}{8} \times 15\frac{1}{4}$ in. (*Rosenwald Collection*). Pl.40

Landscape with Cottage and Hay Barn. Drawing on Paper. $4\frac{1}{8} \times 7$ in. (*Rosenwald Collection*). Pl.140

Portrait of a Lady with an Ostrich-Feather Fan. Canvas. $39\frac{1}{4} \times 32\frac{5}{8}$ in. (*Widener Collection*). Pl.76
Self-Portrait. Canvas. $33\frac{1}{4} \times 26$ in. (*Mellon Collection*). Pl.78
The Mill. Canvas. $34\frac{1}{2} \times 41\frac{1}{2}$ in. (*Widener Collection*). Pl.147

RICCIO (ANDREA BRIOSCO) (1470–1532)
Venus Chastising Cupid. Bronze. $4\frac{3}{16} \times 3\frac{3}{16}$ in. (*Samuel H. Kress Collection*). Pl.41

RIEMENSCHNEIDER, TILMAN (About 1460–1531)
St. Burchard of Würzburg. Wood. $32\frac{3}{8}$ in. high. (*Samuel H. Kress Collection*). Pl.83

ROBBIA, GIROLAMO DELLA (1487–1566)
Effigy of Catherine de' Medici. Louvre, *Paris*. Fig.16

ROBERTI, ERCOLE (About 1456–1496)
Ginevra Bentivoglio. Panel. $21\frac{1}{8} \times 15\frac{1}{4}$ in. (*Samuel H. Kress Collection*). Pl.60

ROSSELLINO, ANTONIO (1427–1478/79)
The Young St. John the Baptist. Marble. $13\frac{5}{8}$ in. high. (*Samuel H. Kress Collection*). Pl.67

ROUSSEAU, HENRI (1844–1910)
The Equatorial Jungle. Canvas. $55\frac{1}{4} \times 51$ in. (*Chester Dale Collection*). Pl.154

RUISDAEL, JACOB VAN (1628/29–1682)
Forest Scene. Canvas. $41\frac{1}{2} \times 51\frac{1}{2}$ in. (*Widener Collection*). Pl.143

SAENREDAM, PIETER JANSZ. (1597–1665)
S. Maria della Febbre, Rome. Panel. $14\frac{7}{8} \times 27\frac{3}{4}$ in. (*Samuel H. Kress Collection*). Pl.157

SCOREL, JAN VAN (1495–1562)
The Rest on the Flight into Egypt. Panel. $22\frac{3}{4} \times 29\frac{1}{2}$ in. (*Samuel H. Kress Collection*). Fig.5; Pl.137

SEBASTIANO DEL PIOMBO (About 1485–1547)
Portrait of a Young Woman as a Wise Virgin. Panel. $21 \times 18\frac{1}{8}$ in. (*Samuel H. Kress Collection*). Pl.68

SIMONE MARTINI (About 1284–1344)
Guidoriccio da Fogliano. Palazzo Pubblico, *Siena*. Fig.9

STEEN, JAN (About 1626–1679)

The Dancing Couple. Canvas. 40⅜ × 56⅛ in. (*Widener Collection*). Pl.108

STUART, GILBERT (1755–1828)

The Skater. Canvas. 96⅝ × 58⅛ in. (*Mellon Collection*). Pl.91

TANZIO DA VARALLO (About 1574–about 1635)

St. Sebastian. Canvas. 46½ × 37 in. (*Samuel H. Kress Collection*). Pl.39

TIEPOLO, GIOVANNI BATTISTA (1696–1770)

Apollo Pursuing Daphne. Canvas. 27 × 34¼ in. (*Samuel H. Kress Collection*). Pl.50

TINTORETTO, JACOPO (1518–1594)

Christ at the Sea of Galilee. Canvas. 46 × 66¼ in. (*Samuel H. Kress Collection*). Pl.37

TITIAN (About 1477–1576)

Doge Andrea Gritti. Canvas. 52 × 41½ in. (*Samuel H. Kress Collection*). Pl.73

Landscape detail of Bellini's Feast of the Gods (Pl.45). (*Widener Collection*). Pl.134

Ranuccio Farnese. Canvas. 35¼ × 29 in. (*Samuel H. Kress Collection*). Pl.75

Venus with a Mirror. Canvas. 49 × 41½ in. (*Mellon Collection*). Pl.47

TURA, COSIMO (About 1430–1495)

Madonna and Child in a Garden. Panel. 20¾ × 14⅝ in. (*Samuel H. Kress Collection*). Pl.35

TURNER, JOSEPH MALLORD WILLIAM (1775–1851)

Keelmen Heaving in Coals by Moonlight. Canvas. 36¼ × 48¼ in. (*Widener Collection*). Pl.148

VELÁZQUEZ, DIEGO (1599–1660)

The Needlewoman. Canvas. 29 × 23⅝ in. (*Mellon Collection*). Pl.114

VERMEER, JAN (1632–1675)

A Woman Weighing Gold. Canvas. 16¾ × 15 in. (*Widener Collection*). Pl.111

A Young Girl with a Flute. Panel. 7⅞ × 7 in. (*Widener Collection*). Pl.80

244

VERROCCHIO, ANDREA DEL (1435–1488)

Putto Poised on a Globe. Painted terra-cotta. 29½ in. high. (*Mellon Collection*). Pl.103

VERROCCHIO, CIRCLE OF, about 1475

Madonna and Child with a Pomegranate. Panel. 6⅛ × 5 in. (*Samuel H. Kress Collection*). Pl.14

VISCHER, PETER THE YOUNGER (1487–1528)

Child on a Dolphin. Bronze. 5¾ in. high. (*Samuel H. Kress Collection*). Pl.104

Orpheus and Eurydice. Bronze. 8 × 5⅞ in. (*Samuel H. Kress Collection*). Pl.42

VOUET, SIMON (1590–1649)

St. Jerome and the Angel. Canvas. 57 × 70¾ in. (*Samuel H. Kress Collection*). Fig.7

WEYDEN, ROGIER VAN DER (1399/1400–1464)

Portrait of a Lady. Panel. 14½ × 10¾ in. (*Mellon Collection*). Pl.59

WHISTLER, JAMES ABBOTT MCNEILL (1834–1903)

L'Andalouse. Canvas. 75¾ × 35¾ in. (*Harris Whittemore Collection*). Pl.88

ZOPPO, MARCO (1433–about 1478)

Madonna and Child. Panel. 15¾ × 11⅝ in. (*Samuel H. Kress Collection*). Pl.13